PRESIDE

Biblical Principles for Personal Growth and
Taking Command of Your Life—A Judge's Verdict

Praise for *Preside*

"*Preside: Biblical Principles for Personal Growth and Taking Command of Your Life—A Judge's Verdict* presents a profound journey into personal empowerment. Authored by the Honorable Reverend Shelyna Brown Hamilton, this book weaves a compelling tapestry from her rich experiences as a lawyer, preacher, and Superior Court judge. Her unique perspective offers creative and liberating insights, providing a fresh view of faith. I wholeheartedly recommend this book to everyone, especially to young women like my daughter and nieces, who can immensely benefit from its profound wisdom. *Preside* is more than a read; it's a journey toward a life redefined by a practical faith that empowers and enriches."

—*Rev. Hurmon Hamilton*
Founding and Senior Pastor
New Beginnings Community Church
Located in the San Francisco Bay Area

"This volume of *Preside*, with its companion guide, serves as a powerful navigation tool to all who seek wisdom to effectively nurture and steward their personal *call* to purpose. This must-read book persuasively empowers persons to engage with the critical thinking needed to experience consistent growth toward responsible and successful living. *Preside* is more than informative and charts a demonstrated path to significant influence. Step-by-step consistent changes offer a blueprint for massive results and increased emotional intelligence.

"Open the covers of this book with a teachable attitude and a mindset for learning and expansion. This is a legacy work capable of crafting generational changes that lead to authentic decision-making by design. Readers will find that the best versions of themselves will be awakened to move forward with initiatives formerly bogged down as lifeless dreams."

—*Dr. Cynthia Rembert James, PhD, DMin*

"Reading and working through *Preside* and the *Preside Companion Guide* was an eye-opening experience—even for a lifelong *church-girl* and hard-driving attorney like me. I naturally desire to *take the wheel* of my life, but the practical, step-by-step approach laid out by Judge Brown in *Preside* helped me slow down and take a deeper look into the principles at work (or not at work) behind the scenes of my past successes (and failures). *Preside* also tackled questions I've had for years, such as, *What exactly is my part as a steward versus God's part as sovereign?* and I gained powerful tools in the Skills section of the book. I'm especially fond of striking thoughts that are not empowering me by saying, *Strike that!* out loud. With all of this, I now feel fully equipped as I move into the next chapter of my abundant, fruitful life."

—*Angenette Frink, Principal Member,*
The Law Offices of A.M. Frink, PLLC
Co-Founder, Dare Divas International, LLC

"*Preside* has been the single most impactful book that I have had the pleasure of reading in the last few years. The principles Judge Brown outlines are full of commonsense wisdom, an outgrowth of her many distinguished years on the bench. In reading and re-reading this work, I was reminded of certain principles and saw new perspectives that I needed to absorb. It has truly been the gift that keeps on giving. So many books in the self-help genre claim to be life-changing and transformative. *Preside* lives up to this claim in the most amazing ways! It's a book that I'll return to again and again to remind myself that I alone must put on my robe and preside over my life with wisdom and intentionality. I cannot recommend this book and Judge Brown's wisdom highly enough! If you want to take control of your life, start here."

—*Davita Joie*

"In her inaugural book *Preside*, Judge Shelyna Brown provides you with a blueprint on how to produce fruitfulness, instead of lack, by being a *Steward* and not a *Spectator* over the plans that God has ordained for your life. She does this by walking you through her own personal journey of being a Superior Court Judge for the State of California and by reinforcing it with practical biblical principles. *Preside* is a great coaching manual for the Christian and Non-Christian alike. I found the book to be motivating, inspiring, challenging, and, in some cases, convicting. It is forcing me to take hard look at my own thought patterns, and it has challenged me to take action. So much so that I plan to read it again!

"If you are ready for a shifting in your life, and you are ready to take full jurisdiction and authority over the plans that God has for you, then make the decision to *Preside*. Remember, 'Never underestimate the power of a decision!'"

—*Andrea Simmonds-Kwakye, Minister, Life Coach*

"Funny, real, and thought-provoking, this book is a must-read for anyone looking for practical tips to improve their well-being and abundance. I love that Judge Shelyna gets down to the nitty-gritty and invites the reader to engage in courageous introspection. She uses the foundation of a basic spiritual principle—Stewardship—with an ingenious twist on courtroom vernacular, to take the reader on a self-help journey to take charge of their life."

—*Shonda Avery, MSW*

"*Preside* is insightful, thought-provoking, and enlightening with a dash of humor—full of wisdom and spiritual nuggets that make us evaluate our positions in life. It encourages everyone to be good stewards of our God-given gifts, to define our jurisdictions, and to *preside* over their lives. *Preside* reminds us that God has already given us the authority. Now, it is our opportunity to exercise it."

—*Deborah Moody*

"Engaging, thoughtful, and thought-provoking, *Preside* has the right balance of spiritual and practical guidance and tools to help you move forward, one step at a time, with taking ownership for your life."
—*J. Sharpe*

"I found this book to be truly inspired by God. For the first time in my life, I could envision what my life would look like if I used the authority that's been afforded me. Several times I had to clench my strands of twenty pearls and thank God the author gave me time for *recess*. I appreciate the author's candid stories that came alive in my heart. I could feel their emotions, joy, and hope. Wholeheartedly, this book has inspired me to re-evaluate my goals and ask myself if they are truly my own or if they are goals I think others want me to pursue. Something unexpected happened when I got to the end of the book. I exhaled and resolved within my heart that no more power would be slated to the crippling and paralyzing beliefs about who I am as a woman, person of color, and who I can be as a leader. I proudly stand and take the oath that when I leave this earth, I am leaving on empty! Everything that God has placed in me can and should be used with joy, intentional stewardship, grace, integrity, and authority. Applying the principles of this book and seeing a change in my life has improved my confidence in making judgments about my life and future! So, it is so ordered—it's time to *Preside!*"
—*Stephany Baker, Assistant Vice President for Community and Culture Office of External Relations, Stanford University*

"Wow! I thoroughly enjoyed reading *Preside* by Shelyna Brown. I became captivated from the very beginning with her thought-provoking teaching and insights. With each chapter, I felt lifted to a positive place of security and realization that God has given me jurisdiction over my own life. He has equipped me to be a wise, resourceful steward and not just a spectator. These words alone were empowering! Her motivational questions and exercises helped counsel me to a place of thought and helped me to be honest with myself. I can dust off my dreams! I am not too old. I can return to school. *Preside* is a valuable life tool that encourages thought, action, and resolution. It is an excellent read with purpose. Thank you, Shelyna!"

—*Charlene Phifer*

"If your life has taken a sidebar, stalled out, or you feel you've reached your full potential—*Preside* is a must-read. This literary genius of knowledge, scripture, and lived experience combined with thoughtful memories that help solidify the formula of stewardship has been priceless. Shelyna reminds us that 'Every journey begins with call.'

"She also tells us, 'Whatever you have right now is enough to accomplish what you were put here on this earth to accomplish.' Many times, we get complacent and allow fear to navigate our movement. *Preside* will empower you to take ownership of your life and the Call so that you begin to invest in you. Again. Thank you for letting God guide you through this project that will surely change lives."

—*Catrina Draper*

"*Preside* is a valuable resource that I use as a reference to help me navigate through my journey in life. From the second I picked up *Preside* to read, I could not put it down because I could identify with the author so well. *Preside* helped me wake up, remember who I am, and reminded me of my purpose and what I was born to accomplish in this lifetime. It also caused me to realize the time frame I have to complete it. God has given us clear instructions on how to navigate through this world, and I finished reading *Preside* with more courage than I ever had before and with the desire to serve at the best of my ability. I love that *Preside* was clear, consist, honest, relatable, and encouraging. After reading *Preside*, I realize that I have been given tangible ways to asses my own thoughts, beliefs, and skills to be stewarded correctly in all areas of my life."

—*Mia Rutherford, owner of Mia's Lash Lab and Mia's Moss*

"*Preside* by retired Judge Shelyna Brown takes you on a walk from the courtroom into an opportunity of a profound call to personal and spiritual empowerment. With seasoned-lawyer wisdom and a compassionate-mentor heart, she creates a transformative journey in this material that shifts you from being a passive spectator to living purposefully as an empowered steward of your life. Judge Brown weaves her compelling personal anecdotes and solid biblical principles to craft a powerful framework for exercising your divine jurisdiction across your life. The book isn't just a wealth of wisdom. With the help of her brilliant worksheets (linked in the book!), you have a toolbox of practical insights and reflective *Recesses* that nudge you to explore and solidify your beliefs, claim and embrace your jurisdiction, and foster an appropriate (abundance) mindset. Whether you're seeking clarity, direction, or a deeper connection with your faith,

Preside stands as a guiding light on a hill. It's more than a short read, because Judge Shelyna equips you to take immediate action every step of the way. I encourage you to step into her compelling invitation and challenge to rise to your calling—and *Preside* over a fulfilled life of grace and JOY."

—*Deni Carruth, Lifestyle and Business Strategist*
Helper of the JOY of Others

"*Preside* by Shelyna is a transformative journey that left me in awe. The author seamlessly weaves her personal experiences into a tapestry of wisdom, guiding readers on a path toward mastering their own lives. Shelyna's writing is not just motivational, but also deeply relatable. Her words resonate with a powerful message—taking charge of our lives and answering the call that God has placed upon us. The author's sincerity is evident as she shares her own journey, making the book feel like a personal conversation with a trusted friend. What sets *Preside* apart is its authenticity. Shelyna's genuine faith and belief in the goodness of God permeate the pages, creating a sense of hope and empowerment for readers. The narrative is not just a collection of self-help advice but a testament to the author's unwavering faith in God's plan."

—*Debra Reyes*

"If you are stuck in your spiritual walk, *Preside* is the book you need. It unravels some of the beliefs we have learned that do not lead to abundant life and creates a path to personal responsibility and a new vision of the sovereignty of God."

—*Kim Henderson*

PRESIDE

Biblical Principles for Personal Growth and
Taking Command of Your Life—A Judge's Verdict

SHELYNA V. BROWN

Capucia LLC
211 Pauline Drive #513
York, PA 17402
www.capuciapublishing.com
Send questions to: support@capuciapublishing.com

Paperback ISBN: 978-1-954920-85-9
eBook ISBN: 978-1-954920-86-6
Library of Congress Control Number: 2024900022

Cover Design: Ranilo Cabo
Layout: Ranilo Cabo
Editor and Proofreader: Simon Whaley
Book Midwife: Carrie Jareed

Printed in the United States of America

Capucia LLC is proud to be a part of the Tree Neutral® program. Tree Neutral offsets the number of trees consumed in the production and printing of this book by taking proactive steps such as planting trees in direct proportion to the number of trees used to print books. To learn more about Tree Neutral, please visit treeneutral.com.

This book is dedicated to all who came before me. My relatives and ancestors are the pillars of strength and resilience upon which I stand.

To my grandparents, who weathered the storms of segregation and discrimination, you taught me the true meaning of perseverance and courage. Your stories of triumph over adversity have fueled my determination to break down barriers and pave the way for others.

To my parents, who instilled in me the values of service and the relentless pursuit of knowledge, your guidance and love have been my guiding light.

To my ancestors, whose struggles and sacrifices have created a path for generations to come, I honor your memory by living your dreams.

I am acutely aware that my achievements would not have been possible without your unwavering support, sacrifice, and enduring legacy.

Thank you for making it possible for my dreams to become a reality.

CONTENTS

FOREWORD

It is an honor to introduce you to a powerful and insightful book by retired Judge Shelyna Brown. She brings her experience in the courtroom and relates it to governing our lives so we can reach our God-given potential. I had the privilege of pastoring Judge Brown for over thirty years, watching her ascend from a law student to the bench of the Superior Court of Santa Clara. I'm honored to have been a part in her spiritual growth over that time and to continue to be a part of the next chapter of her life.

Her insight on the principles of stewardship, jurisdiction, and mindset will lead you in fresh new ways to achieve life goals that have otherwise been placed on the backburner of dreams deferred.

As you embark on this literary journey, you will find an amazing and challenging path to broadening your understanding of the *hows* and *whys* of presiding over your life and destiny. I encourage you to buckle up and prepare for a complete transformation of your life as the information and insight within this book will undoubtedly leave a lasting impact.

—Dr. Tony Williams, Founder and Pastor Emeritus
Bay Area Maranatha Christian Center and Maranatha
Outreach Center

INTRODUCTION

For over a decade, I was a Superior Court Judge. During that time, I presided over tens of thousands of cases. To *preside* means to occupy a place of authority or to be in charge of something. It means that you have been given the authority and responsibility to direct and guide proceedings. It is important, however, to understand that a judge is merely the steward of the proceedings.

A judge takes an oath that she will not do anything outside of the boundaries and laws set by the government. When a judge dons the robe, everything she does in the courtroom is on behalf of the government she represents. All of her authority and resources come from that government. She also has the full backing of her government. There are provisions and remedies if and when mistakes are made. The judge's goal, at all times, is to maintain order and get a just outcome for those involved. It is an awesome and sometimes daunting position, but it is also very rewarding and fulfilling.

After several years of exercising this incredible authority, I noticed that when I was in my courtroom, robed, and seated on the bench, I was confident about what I was supposed to do at all times. I knew what I could and could not do. I handled every task put before me, and I didn't waste time on things outside of my jurisdiction.

I understood and carried out the duty to handle and make decisions on every task put before me without fear. I listened to complex arguments and made difficult decisions that affected people's lives more times than I could count each day. I listened to the most horrific and heart-wrenching stories and made rulings without allowing my emotions to get the best of me. I felt confident making decisions and managed any problem or situation, no matter how difficult, how emotional, or how high the stakes were. Whatever was happening, I created and maintained order for my courtroom and, more importantly, for myself.

There was a time when my private life wasn't going quite this well. We have all experienced being fruitful in some areas of our lives and suffering total lack in others. Perhaps your career is going well, but one or more of your relationships are in shambles (this was me). Or maybe your relationship is great, but you are not growing spiritually. Well, I began to wonder why I felt so empowered on the bench and yet so helpless in certain areas of my personal life.

Over many years of presiding over some heinous and complex cases, I discovered a biblical principle that changed everything for me. It is the *Principle of Stewardship*. I know, whenever we think of stewardship, we think of managing money, our time, or our talents. However, this biblical principle is much broader than that. It has empowered me to navigate areas where I was once stuck and all I could do was pray and wait on the Lord to do something... anything. Sometimes, I waited for years or even decades.

There are certainly times when you should wait on the Lord. I have learned the hard way what happens when you don't, so I'm not suggesting moving ahead of God or being outside of His will in any way. But there is a way to be a good steward of everything in our lives, including the wait. Wouldn't it be amazing if there were a biblical principle that allowed us to be as confident as a judge and empowered to make decisions without fear? And what if that principle gave us the clarity to know exactly when to move and when to wait on the Lord?

That's what I want to share with you in this book: The Principle of Stewardship. We know from the Parable of the Ten Talents that good stewards are fruitful and poor stewards suffer from lack. I want to share with you how to steward and be fruitful in every area of your life. Understanding the awesome power of stewardship gives us the confidence to preside over the areas that we should, the patience to wait on God when we should, and the wisdom to know the difference. The result is fruitfulness and abundance in areas where we have suffered from lack for years and maybe even decades.

The Principle of Stewardship is a game-changer. You will no longer be a spectator of your life, just waiting to see what happens. Empowered by God as a good steward over your life, you will manage a fruitful and abundant life. Understanding this principle will change the way you see God and the way you see yourself. I find it interesting that so many of us grew up being afraid of God, too scared to make decisions because we were taught and believed that He was just waiting for us to make a mistake so He could punish us. This is despite our constant declarations that God is good. The Principle of Stewardship reveals that God is a gracious and loving God who encourages us and even requires us to be good stewards. What I'm saying is that despite what we've heard and sung about in church, God is not in control of our lives. Yes, God is sovereign. We will see that, in His sovereignty, He bestowed to us authority and responsibility to steward our own lives. That does not mean He is not there for us, leading and guiding us. It means that we have a part to play. "The heart of man plans his way, but the LORD establishes his steps" (Proverbs 16:9 ESV). God is always faithful to do His part. The question is, are we doing our part?

The idea of stewarding and making decisions about what you want to do, be, or have may sound a bit scary. After all, when you are a steward, there is no one to blame. But I promise, if you go with me on this journey of stewardship, I will lay out all the facts that prove that we are all called to stewardship. Through scripture, I will show you that God not only wants you to steward your life, but He also requires you to do so. Through my journey of becoming a judge and thus the ultimate steward, I share with you the steps required to become a steward. This is so crucial to know because we know good stewards are fruitful. Being fruitful is good for us, but it also glorifies God.

I will share how my journey to presiding in a court of law has allowed me to use those same principles and tools to become a good steward of my entire life. To become a judge, it all starts with the call. After the call, you must take an oath. After the oath, you are qualified to don the judge's robe. After the robe, you must receive training on the laws and principles that you will be using. Once you take the bench, you have all the authority you need to rule on any matter that comes before you. When you become the judge and are seated on the bench with authority, you are no longer a spectator. You are a steward. If you could have the confidence of a judge to know exactly what to do in any situation, when to rule or when to wait, wouldn't you want to exercise that authority? Well, as a steward, you can. You will understand the authority, the jurisdiction, the mindset, the heartset, or beliefs, and the skill set that will allow you to preside over your life. You have the power to choose a life of lack or one of abundance. Which will you choose?

How to Use This Book

My goal with this book is to take you on a journey from being a spectator to being a steward in every area of your life. Each chapter addresses a principle or idea that you should master to be a good steward.

Throughout the book, I've provided a time of reflection that I call a *recess*. A recess is a short break in a legal proceeding. It allows all the participants an opportunity to take a break to regroup or refresh. It also allows participants to gather their thoughts and prepare for the next session. I've designed these recesses as an opportunity for you to reflect and go deeper with questions and worksheets. They will help you master each principle of the journey and build upon them. You may want to do them as you go along or return to them after you have finished the book in its entirety. Or you may decide to skip these exercises altogether. Do what works best for you. You are the steward of your journey.

One last thing, the principles and tools that I discuss in this book are universal. However, I view them through my personal faith in Christ Jesus. You can apply these principles if you are a person of a different faith or of no faith or religion.

I have developed exercises to help you work through some of the chapters. Download and print your exercises now by going to:

shelynabrown.com/preside-thebookworksheets

CHAPTER I

The Call to Judgeship

It was 2010, and it was close to Christmas. I was finishing up my errands before heading home from work. My dashboard lit up with an incoming call. I didn't recognize the area code, so I was tempted just to let it go to voicemail. But curiosity got the better of me, so I answered it.

A male voice said, "Hi, this is J.G. Is this Shelyna Brown?" His voice sounded familiar, but I couldn't recall from where. He'd also pronounced my name right, which made me think he knew me. I always know when it's a telemarketer because they mispronounce my name, *Shell-na*. I wasn't sure who it was or what it was about, so I used my work voice.

"Hello, this Shelyna."

"This is J.G. I'm calling from the governor's office. I would like to let you know the governor has chosen to appoint you to the bench in Santa Clara County. I'm calling to see if you will accept the appointment."

There was complete silence. I was trying to process the words.

I must have been silent for a second too long because he said, "Hello?"

It jolted me back to reality. *You're kidding*, I thought. Although, I guess I said it out loud because he chuckled.

"I wouldn't kid about something like that," he replied.

"Let me pull over. I don't want to crash." I'm not sure why I said that either. I could have just pulled over. I could no longer distinguish between what I was thinking and what I was saying out loud.

He was patient. I quickly pulled over and asked again, "Are you serious?"

He assured me I was not dreaming and again asked if I would accept the appointment. I'm not sure if I said, screamed, or sang my response. All I know is that I said, "Absolutely YES!" The last thing I remember saying was, "Thank you, thank you, thank you, thank you!"

I had waited for this day for nearly four years. It was never my plan to be a judge. This was my exceedingly abundant moment.

Four years earlier, I was teaching at a women's conference, and one of the more seasoned women in the class pulled me aside. She said, "I know you're a lawyer, but have you ever thought about being a judge?"

Uh no, I thought. *I'm a Public Defender. They never get appointed, and I don't have any money to run an election.* "No," I replied.

"When you were speaking," she continued, "all I could see was you as a judge. You speak with authority and people want to listen to you."

I just looked at her. My heart was pounding, but I didn't know what to say. She hugged me, wished me well, and said a prayer over me, and she was gone. Was this a prophetic word? She seemed to be so sure. I thought about it all day and even wrote it in my journal. It felt like such a profound moment. I wanted to believe her, but I just couldn't.

From that moment on, every time I went into a courtroom, which was once in the morning and once in the afternoon, every day, I would try to imagine myself sitting on the bench. How would I rule? What would I say in difficult moments? Judges always seemed to know exactly what to say and what to do. I couldn't do that. She must have gotten her prophetic wires crossed. I was working in my dream job, making good money. I was fine.

Sidebar: Like every journey, the journey to preside begins with a call. A call is an invitation to do something you've never done before, experience something you've never experienced before, or become something you've only dreamed of being.

A few weeks later, a judge who I admire called me to the bench. I thought I was in trouble because I had pushed back, maybe a little too hard, on a ruling he had made earlier. But he asked me to come to his chambers after the session. I stood at the door, waiting for him to invite me in. After I sat down, he said, "Have you ever thought about putting your name in for appointment to the bench?"

I just looked at him. This was a joke, right? "Uh, no," I responded. "You know they never appoint public defenders."

He acted like he didn't hear me and continued, "I've been observing you, and I think you would make a good judicial officer."

To be honest, I don't really remember the rest of the conversation. My mind had gone back to the conversation I had weeks earlier. Was this some crazy conspiracy?

A few months later, some judicial slots opened up, and it seemed that everywhere I went, people were asking if I was going to apply for a judicial appointment. I thought about it, prayed about it, and decided to discuss it with my family and close friends. Surely, they would think it ridiculous, and I could forget about it.

My father said, "Pipsy, I can totally see you on the bench."

One of my friends from high school even reminded me that I'd mentioned becoming a judge in passing. I have to tell you, I don't ever remember musing about being a judge.

Finally, I did it. I downloaded the application, but it took me three months to fill it out. It took me another three months to build up enough courage to ask colleagues and other judges to write letters of support. I did several interviews, and the grapevine told me I was doing really well in the process. Family and friends at church were praying for me and claiming victory. It seemed that all was going well until the night they announced seven judges had been selected, even one from my office, but I was not one of them. I was shocked!

What happened? I had a great amount of support from my colleagues and several judges. I even had the support of opposing counsel, some of whom even wrote unsolicited letters of support. I felt so embarrassed and inadequate. Remember, I had to go back to work with all these people who now knew I had aspirations for the bench. I had to endure holidays where people wanted to know what happened. Most of the people were kind, but a few seemed to enjoy the fact that I had failed. This wasn't fair. I didn't even know I had a desire to be a judge until that woman pulled me aside with her prophetic words. I felt God had set me up to fail, to look like a fool. It took some time, but I had to decide what I believed about God. Did I really believe He was a good God? Would a good God set me up to fail? Or would a good God teach me that failing was a part of the journey? I had to decide if I really believed that all things are always working for my good, and that included the failures and the setbacks. Well, I can confidently say yes. I do believe that all things are working for me. And a year later, here I was, parked crooked and smiling. J.G. gave me a few more instructions and hung up.

Becoming a judge was my Ephesians 3:20 moment: "Now to him who is able to do far more abundantly than all that we ask or think, according to the power at work within us" (ESV). For as long as I can remember, I always wanted to be a lawyer. I had the privilege of serving as an attorney with the Office of the Public Defender for fifteen years. There, I served the indigent, those with addiction, mental health issues, and other marginalized groups. It was often a thankless job, but I loved it. When someone first suggested that I become a judge, I literally laughed at the idea. I did not think that it was possible. But God created an opportunity for me and, over a decade later, I can only say that becoming a judge was exceedingly and abundantly above anything I could ask or even think of. It is an incredible honor that the State of California entrusted me with the power to administer justice to the citizens of Santa Clara County. It was a great privilege and an even greater responsibility.

RECESS

We are always being called to something more.
What are you being called to?
Have you answered the call?
If not, why not?

CHAPTER 2

A Greater Call

Before the call from the governor's office, the most important call of my life came when I was in the fourth grade. By then, I was very familiar with church. I grew up in the church. No, I mean, I *literally* grew up in the church. Sunday started with Sunday School at 9:00 a.m. There was a break for breakfast, and then church at 10:45 a.m. Often there was a 3:00 p.m. service. We would rush home to get something to eat and maybe take a nap. Back then, we had real Sunday dinners. A roast, not in an Instant Pot or even a Crockpot. A pot roast, in a pot that was put in the oven before we left for church, with real mashed potatoes, fresh green beans we snapped the day before, and homemade rolls. I still wonder how our mothers and grandmothers had the time to cook all of that from scratch when they were in church all day. Anyway, after that, it was back to the Young People's Willing Workers' (YPWW) meeting at 6:30 p.m., followed by the night service, which began at 7:30 p.m. I would often sneak to the back of the church to do my homework when the evening service began. It's a wonder any of us graduated with this rigorous church schedule.

The rest of the week was no better. We usually had Monday night off, unless there was a special pageant or service to prepare for.

Bible study was on Wednesday, choir rehearsal on Thursday, and youth night on Friday. The ushers practiced, the Sunshine Band met, and some auxiliaries (now they are called ministries) were always selling dinners, washing cars, or just cleaning the church. If there was a revival, all bets were off, and we were just in church every night. I'm not kidding when I say I grew up inside the church.

I knew what to wear and how to act in church. I knew the exact time to wave your hand or when to shout out, "Amen!" or "Preach!" My cousin Kim and I even mastered how to pass notes during prayer, without getting caught—no easy feat. I loved watching the saints catch the Holy Ghost and start shoutin'. To this day, if the shoutin' music starts, I look for a tambourine to accompany the saints as they dance.

But looking back on it now, what I didn't have was what the saints called a personal relationship with God. I think this is because the church I attended talked a lot about where you would go after you died. Like most kids, I never really thought about dying, or that I could die. I was just a kid. What I didn't understand at the time is how my relationship with God could help me live a more abundant and satisfying life right then.

Well, one day, one of my friends at school had a pamphlet that said the world was going to end. For whatever reason, I believed it. All those messages about heaven and hell came flooding back to me. I realized that, if I died at that moment, I didn't know if I would go to heaven or hell. I did the only thing I could think of. I called my grandmother.

My grandmother was what we call a Mother of the Church. Her nickname was Sister Kitchen. Yes, because she could burn. She always brought the potato salad that everybody ate. Whenever I think of my grandmother, mostly what I remember is her cooking, praying, or reading her Bible. I trusted that if anyone would know what to do with my twelve-year-old soul, she would. I thought about it all day. What if this prophecy was true and the world just ended while I was on the bus on the way home? When I finally got home, I called Gram at the church, because that was where she always was, cooking, reading her Bible, and/or praying.

"Hello, Faith Evangel Church of God in Christ."

I knew her voice immediately. "Gram, Stephanie had a pamphlet that said the world was going to end this year."

I don't remember exactly what else I said, but I remember being a little panicked when I told her about how the world was going to end.

She just listened, and when I was done, she said, "What does the Bible say?"

That was her answer for everything. I was silent. I didn't know what the Bible said. I just knew I was scared.

"Ok," she said. "I'll be down to the house directly."

That meant she was coming to pick me up. Our house was only a short walk from the church. Within fifteen minutes, she pulled into the driveway in her faded yellow Chevy Nova hatchback and blew her horn. I ran out and got in the car. I didn't know where we were going but, if the world was going to end, I wanted to be with my grandmother. She was the most righteous and faithful person I knew. If anybody was going to heaven, she was, and I wanted to go with her. I handed her the pamphlet. She barely looked at it and handed it back to me.

"Chile, don't you know? No man knows the day or the hour when Christ will return."

I knew she was quoting scripture because she was always quoting scripture, but I didn't know what it meant.

She drove around the neighborhood and picked up Sister Morris and Mother Tarkington, prayer warriors she called them, and we went down to the church. We all kneeled on the altar and they sang and prayed for a while. There was no music and each of these women was chanting a different prayer. I just listened to the familiar voices, and I felt comforted.

"Do you know Jesus?" Gram asked me.

"Yes, I think so."

"Then why are you scared?"

I didn't have an answer. I just looked at her with tears in my eyes.

"There's no reason to be scared. When you know Jesus, you're safe in His arms and nothing can harm you. Do you want to know Jesus?"

I nodded. My grandmother then led me in the Prayer of Salvation. I repeated words I'd heard in church my entire life, but this time, I heard them and accepted them with my heart. The other ladies said the words with me. Then they each hugged me, and they continued praying and singing. I just sat on that altar thinking about what this would mean for me when I died, but also what it would mean for me tomorrow at school. How would this change how I lived every day?

On that random Tuesday night, at Faith Evangel Church of God in Christ (COGIC), I was surrounded by ladies, the mothers of the church, who took the time to lead me to the throne of grace, and I accepted Christ as my personal savior. After that night, I was sure I knew Jesus.

Since that time, I have embraced the teachings of Christ and have become a student of the word of God. I was licensed as a minister in 2008. I believe God's grace saved me when I confessed my sins. I have seen several pamphlets and magazine covers in the grocery store that predict the end of the world. I always look at them and smile. I remember that night, years ago, and know that no matter what happens, I am safe in the arms of Jesus.

If you are a follower of Jesus Christ, then you have already accepted the most important call. You have accepted Christ as your savior. When did you accept the call? For some of you, it may have been recently. For others, it may have been years or even decades ago. It is worth remembering when we first received the call and how we responded. If you can't remember, you can and should reaffirm your commitment to be a follower of Christ.

If you haven't accepted the call, you can accept it right now. It should be a free and voluntary decision. It is not something you do because your parents wanted you to or because you have been in church your whole life. Know that Christ loved you so much that He chose you from the foundation of the earth. "Even before he made the world, God loved us and chose us in Christ to be holy and without fault in his eyes" (Ephesians 1:4 NLT).

Before you can exercise your kingdom's authority properly, you must answer the call. You must choose Him. There is no time like the present. If you have someone who can lead you in a prayer of salvation, put down this book and call them. If you do not know anyone, I invite you to go to the appendix of this book and pray the Prayer of Salvation. Welcome to the family!

When I was licensed as a minister, my pastor, Dr. Tony Williams, said, "When God called you to ministry, He first calls you to Himself." Before Christ sends us on any journey, He calls us to Himself. It's where we learn of His love and grace and where He equips us for the journey. Answering the call says that you accept Jesus Christ as your savior. This is the most important decision I've ever made. Not just because it let me have peace about where I would spend eternity, but also determined the kind of life that I could live here on earth. A life where there is grace, peace, and new mercies every day. It is a beautiful life. It is also the first step to the abundant life that you desire and deserve.

I share my conversion story with you, not just because I wanted you to know more about me and where I come from, but also because it is the first and most crucial step in this process called *Preside*. Like you, I've had to answer so many other calls: the call to higher education, the call to becoming a responsible adult and a reliable friend, and a lawyer. It goes on and on. Every decision I made to answer each of those calls put me on the path to who I have become. I look forward to the call that propels me to who I will become next.

RECESS

Take a few moments to review your conversion story or a time
when you felt called to something greater. Write it down.
Do you remember when you first sensed
the call of God or a higher power?
If yes, was it a free and voluntary decision or
did you do so because it was expected of you?
How do you feel when you think back on this story?

CHAPTER 3

Beliefs

Every journey begins with a call. But if we don't believe in our heart that we can be successful on the journey, then many of us won't even take the first step. The state of our heart, what we believe, is just as important as our mindset and our skill set. Even if we venture out, but we don't really believe we will succeed, we do so half-heartedly and without confidence. Our beliefs become a self-fulfilling prophecy of our ill-fated attempt to make the journey.

A belief is having the utmost confidence that something is true. It's an opinion that you have thought about so many times you no longer consider whether or not it's true. Just like a judge's order, you follow it because you have to.

Beliefs influence everything in our lives. We have everything we believe we can have and nothing more. If we don't believe we are worthy of the lifestyle, the relationship, or the abundance that we pray for, we won't be able to receive it.

There are many beliefs that will help you along any journey. However, there are two essential beliefs that we must have on this journey from being a Spectator to becoming a Steward:

1) God is good: Psalm 34:8, 107:1, 145:9 (ESV),
2) All things are working out for me: Romans 8:28 (ESV).

This journey of life is not always easy, and many obstacles and setbacks are sure to come your way. But if you hold on to the fact that God is good all the time, and that He wants for you to have a life and have it more abundantly, it will make even the toughest situations easier to bear. If you believe that a lifetime of suffering and lack is God's will for you, you may have to re-evaluate whether or not you truly believe God is good. If you believe that God can work everything for your good, even your failures and missteps, you can weather any journey. Your beliefs will keep you going even when all looks like it's lost. We must be good stewards of what we believe.

It took me a long time to apply for a judicial appointment. I just could not see it. I didn't believe it could happen for me. I had to pray about it, seek wise counsel, and discover what the Bible said about what I could do before I could really believe it. It wasn't until I believed it was possible that I was able to make the first step toward that goal. We cannot live beyond our beliefs.

Powerful Beliefs

Behind everything we do or don't do, there exists a powerful or paralyzing belief. A *paralyzing* belief produces lack—the opposite of what we want. A *powerful* belief produces fruit, despite facts and data. My mother tells me that at my first-grade graduation, I announced I would become a lawyer. I was standing on the stage at the end of the line, right in front of George, the tallest kid in our class. We were outfitted in white caps and gowns. I remember that day, the first of many graduations. I also remember standing in line and being excited as the teacher went down the line asking each of us what we wanted to be when we grew up.

According to my mother, the answers were typical: a ballerina, a basketball player, a nurse, etc. I remember that day, and that the cap and gown were white with little blue and pink cap-and-gown motifs on them, but I don't remember my answer to the teacher's question.

However, my Mom remembers she was shocked when I said in a clear voice that I was going to be a lawyer. We didn't have any lawyers in our family, in our neighborhood, or at our church. She wondered how I even knew what a lawyer was!

> **Sidebar: "And Jesus said to him, 'If you can'! All things are possible for one who believes."**
> **(Mark 9:23 ESV)**

To be honest, I don't know how I knew that either. I believe God dropped that desire in my heart because I honestly can't think of anything else I've ever wanted to be. I had a powerful belief. I remember, in the second or third grade, we had professionals come in and talk to us about their jobs. I remember there was a lawyer. I don't know what kind of law she practiced, but she said that their job was to help people. She said that lawyers help people get justice in court. I was sold. I didn't know exactly what justice was, but it sounded good to me. I knew, then and there, sitting criss-crosssed on the floor of Ms. Markarian's classroom, that I would become a lawyer. I had no idea of the obstacles I would face or that statistics dictated it was unlikely that someone from my neighborhood could become a lawyer. I just believed it and that was it. Maybe that's why the Bible says that unless we "become like little children, you will never enter the kingdom of heaven" (Matthew 18:3 NIV). Children have the audacity to believe beyond what looks impossible.

Recall a powerful belief—a place where you experience abundance.
What were the results of maintaining that powerful belief? What
obstacles did you overcome to maintain this belief?
Do you have a childhood dream with a powerful belief you can revisit?

Paralyzing Beliefs

Beliefs can also be paralyzing. Paralyzing beliefs produce lack. A paralyzing belief I once had centered on marriage and relationships. Based on what I observed and experienced in my home, my neighborhood, and my church, I developed certain beliefs about what it meant to be in a relationship or to be married. Somehow, I associated being a successful lawyer as incompatible with being married. This was grounded in what I heard people say about marriage. I knew women who no longer went after their dreams after they married. Some even hid their talents, gifting, or how much money they made from their significant other. Ultimately, I developed an erroneous belief that I could have one thing: a successful career as a lawyer or a marriage, but not both. I wasn't willing to give up my dream of being a lawyer for anyone, and I'm unsure what inspired the belief that I had to. That's the thing about beliefs: they don't have to be true to be paralyzing.

I remember noticing at a young age that women had the responsibility of caring for the kids and doing most of the work in the home. This was true in my own home. My dad was a great cook, but it was my mom who cooked most of the time. But one of my fondest memories was of Sunday mornings when my dad would cook while Lionel Richie's *Easy Like Sunday Morning* played in the background, and the smell of bacon, eggs, and biscuits wafted through the house.

Despite the somewhat joint effort, it was still my mom who did the lion's share of the housework while also holding down a job. I remember my mom and dad arguing about my mom going back to school to get her degree. My mom eventually went back and got her bachelor's degree, and then her master's degree, but it caused a lot of conflict.

Sidebar: Believing something does not make it true.

This belief was reinforced at church, where I always heard that the man is the head of the house and the provider, and the woman should just submit. What my young ears heard was that being married meant the woman had to be smaller, beneath, or less than the man. This, of course, is not true, but no one ever explained that the previous verse to the one they were quoting says that husbands and wives should "Submit to one another out of reverence for Christ," Ephesians 5:21 (NLT). Nor did they explain and elaborate that we are all created equal in the eyes of Christ. "There is neither Jew nor Greek, there is neither slave nor free, there is neither male nor female; for you are all one in Christ Jesus," (Galatians 3:28 NKJV).

Nevertheless, this is what I heard and what I believed. Everything I saw and experienced seemed to support this belief. Well-meaning church mothers and play cousins would tell me they were proud of me for going and getting an education. But they also said I should get married before I got too much education because "You know how men are." I always smiled, but I didn't know what they meant.

The reinforcement that having too much money, education, or being too much was a death blow to any shred of belief I had that I could marry. Male mentors and advisors would joke that I had climbed that ladder too high and would not likely find a mate, and maybe that was just my cross to bear. I was once told by a male colleague that I was more likely to be struck by lightning than to marry a suitable man if I continued focusing on my career. Many of these words were spoken by people whom I love and/or admire. This only further fueled my belief, whether or not it was true.

Far too often, I saw friends and family members enter relationships, or marry, forfeiting their dreams in the process. They'd stop pursuing an advanced degree or downplay their success just to keep the peace.

Of course, I certainly saw healthy relationships where the pair was equally yoked. It's just that when you have a belief, you fall into a cycle of confirmation bias. That is where you only focus on the things that confirm and enforce what you already believe and you ignore all other data.

Beliefs have more influence and impact than we realize. Beliefs determine what we can receive. In Matthew 13, Jesus returned to His hometown to teach. While many were amazed by His wisdom and miraculous powers, Jesus did not do many miracles in that town because of their unbelief. Jesus was still Jesus and could still perform miracles. It was their limiting beliefs about who they thought Jesus was and what He could do that limited their ability to receive miracles that were available to them. It wasn't until I began to preside over this belief and steward this area that I was able to have a beautiful and healthy relationship.

RECESS

Recall a paralyzing belief—a place where you are experiencing lack.

Where did this paralyzing belief come from?

Is that belief true?

What has been the result of that paralyzing belief?

What can you now do to turn that paralyzing belief into a powerful one?

To help with this exercise, download a copy of the Preside Over Your Beliefs (Belief Wheel) Worksheet by going to: shelynabrown.com/preside-thebookworksheets

How Do I Know What I Believe?

The right beliefs are like rocket fuel to our dreams. It's important to know what we believe so we can know where we're headed. In coaching, counseling, or ministry, I often try to help people discover what they really believe about what they are trying to achieve. When I was hoping to be a judge, I had to re-evaluate some of my beliefs. I was a young public defender, (forty-one years old), and a single black woman with no children. That didn't exactly fit the mold of what people, including myself, usually thought about what a judge should be. I had to believe that I was worthy of sitting on that bench and that God would give me everything I needed to do the job with excellence. It wasn't easy, but eventually, I got my beliefs to align with God's idea of what I could do and who I could become.

There are at least two ways to discover the difference between what you *say* you believe and what you *truly* believe:

1) Making preparations, and
2) The stories we tell.

Making Preparations

When I was in high school, we had to check in with our counselor to discuss our career plans. This was a no-brainer for me. Ever since that first-grade graduation, I was determined to be a lawyer. I just believed I could. That belief fueled me through grammar school, junior high, and high school. Everything I did, the classes I took, the grades I strived for, staying out of trouble—all of it was motivated by this belief in my future as a lawyer. I didn't know it at the time, but I was being a good steward of my beliefs. My classmates made fun of me for being a nerd. Some teachers and counselors thought my declaration was too ambitious, but nothing could sway me.

As high school juniors, we were assigned a counselor to help us to plan for college. I was happy to be assigned to Ms. Em. She was an advisor to the student government where I was an officer, so I interacted with her often and had a good rapport with her. I remember that she was always well-dressed, and her hair always looked like Clair Huxtable's from *The Cosby Show*. She was always very nice to me, so I was somewhat taken aback by her reaction to my future plans.

"Shelyna, your grades are good, and you've taken all the college prep classes. Do you know where you want to go to college and what you want to be?"

I had just finished the University of California (UC) college tours, and I said confidently, "I'm going to UC Davis and I'm going to be a lawyer."

She didn't smile as I expected. Whenever I told a family member, they smiled broadly and agreed that I would be a lawyer. My grandmother especially would always say, "I believe you will be a lawyer 'cuz you're always talkin' and you ask too many questions." My favorite was, "You will argue with a stop sign."

Ms. Em, on the other hand, pursed her lips and said slowly, "That's good. But I know your dad is a teacher and your mom is a social worker. Have you thought about those careers?"

I just looked at her. Did she not hear me?

"I'm going to be a lawyer," I repeated.

"Okay, that's going to take a lot of work, and it is a very challenging career. I just want you to think about something that you can really do."

I didn't say anything else. I just sat there with my arms crossed, waiting to be excused. *She doesn't believe that I can become a lawyer, but I'll show her!*

Admittedly, when I reflected on this experience previously, I would get upset. How could she pour cold water on my dreams like that? However, when I think about it now, I don't believe she meant any harm. I realize, or at least I like to believe, that she liked me and wanted me to succeed. I imagine she had probably seen countless kids from my neighborhood try to do big things and fail. Selecting a career that we were all familiar with was safe. It was more likely that I could become a teacher or social worker rather than have the lofty goal of becoming an attorney. I often tell young people I mentor, and now I'm telling you, it is okay to be unreasonable and unrealistic in your dreams. That's what dreams are for. No one else has to understand it or believe it, as long as you believe it.

I left Ms. Em's office quietly. I was a little shaken, but even more determined to achieve my goal. I chose this time to steward my belief and not let it wither under someone else's opinion or belief about who I could become. I went home and did what I always did when somebody dared to doubt me and my dream: I unpacked and re-packed a travel trunk I had purchased for college. I had picked the colors of my dorm room, peach and white, and I already had towels, sheets, and quarters for laundry packed away. It didn't matter that I had not yet been accepted into any college. At that point, I hadn't even applied to any colleges, and I had no idea how I would afford it. But I was preparing to go to college, the first step on my journey to becoming a lawyer.

Preparation is the easiest way to determine what it is you believe. If you are preparing, despite what your circumstances may look like or what other people are saying, you are stewarding, or *presiding*, over your belief. I did attend UC Davis and college went pretty smoothly, but I was not accepted to the first law school of my choice. However, I never stopped packing my trunk. I knew that I would be accepted somewhere. I ended up at Santa Clara University School of Law (SCU). It wasn't easy or perfect. I completely blew my first law school exam. My roommate, Kristi, seemed calm and confident as we drove home from that exam. I was shaken. I still have no idea what Father Goda was asking on that contracts exam, but despite my rough start, I had the best experience in law school. I made enduring friendships and I go back to SCU to mentor students and teach as often as I can. I was sworn in as a judge at SCU, the place where I failed my first law school exam. Through all the setbacks and disappointments, I believed all things were working for me. We get what we prepare for. When I look back, I realize that for years I had been preparing to be a judge. I learned and honed my craft as an attorney. I'd practiced law with integrity. I studied judges every time I was in court, watching what they did, how they interacted with staff and litigants, and listening not just to what they said but how they said it. I was ready.

What are you preparing for? What have you packed in your trunk?

RECESS

What do you say you believe about_____?
How are you preparing for it?
If you're not preparing for it, why not?
What is one thing you can do to prepare for it?

The Stories We Tell

"Death and life are in the power of the tongue, and those who love it will eat its fruits," (Proverbs 18:21 ESV).

Another way to understand what we believe is by the stories we tell. I don't know if you've noticed this, but when we are talking with others, we often tell stories. We learn these stories from what we have seen and heard throughout our lives. We interpret what we are experiencing and give meaning to what we see, hear, and experience. Then we tell stories based on that interpretation. The stories we tell reveal what we really believe. Are you still telling the story about the breakup ten years ago or how unfair they were to you at your job? We speak life or death with our stories. You may not have even noticed it, but many of our stories are about the lack we have seen or experienced, the defeats we have experienced, or the obstacles ahead that are keeping us from our dreams and goals. A story that speaks life is a story that talks about the possibilities, not the obstacles. If you really want to know what you believe about a certain topic, listen to the stories you are telling:

- "You know I was going to go back to school, but there are no programs to fit my schedule or budget."

- "I would like to date, but there are no good men/women in this city."
- "I would try for that job, but you know 'they' won't ever let me have that position."
- "I don't trust myself. I always choose the wrong person."

One thing I've learned as a judge is that just because something is true, it may not be relevant. It might be true that for 232 years there wasn't an African American woman sitting on the highest court in the land. But that was not relevant to Supreme Court Justice, Ketanji Brown Jackson. It may be true that you failed before, but is it relevant to what you can and will do in the future? The next time you're with your friends, listen to the stories you are hearing and telling. I did a challenge with the ladies from my church a few years ago. It was a five-day challenge to speak only life. I challenge you to do the same. Find an accountability partner and practice only speaking words that are affirming and line up with the word of God for five days. Take notes each day about where you encountered difficulties. Is it when speaking about work, a relationship, a situation, or speaking about yourself? I encourage you to tell a new story. Try it.

RECESS

What are some of the stories you have been telling?
Are they stories of abundance or stories of lack?
Will you commit to the five-day Speak Life Challenge?

To help with this exercise, download a copy of the Stories We Tell Worksheet by going to: shelynabrown.com/preside-thebookworksheets

CHAPTER 4

Principles

Discover the Principles You Will Need for This Journey.

One way God chose to lead and guide us is with principles. A principle is a consistent rule that governs how something was created to operate. Every government, society, organization, or institution has its own rules about how it will be governed. Unlike man-made laws, God's principles are immutable. Remember, there was a time not too long ago when the Jim Crow laws and interning Japanese Americans were not only legal but considered moral. Principles don't change based on culture or society. They govern exactly the same way, no matter where they are in the world or who is exercising them.

Where did these principles come from? All of these principles were established by God. God created the world and everything in it. He established principles to govern everything in the natural and the spiritual worlds. Throughout time, humanity discovered the principles and gave them names. The principles of gravity, aerodynamics, or Archimedes' Principle of Buoyancy were not *created* by humanity but were merely discovered and named by humanity.

Sidebar: Many of the principles that we know from the Bible are also referenced in other religions and/or disciplines. These are often called universal or spiritual principles. For the sake of this discussion, I am referring to them as Biblical Principles.

So why did God establish principles? Principles bring order to chaos. God is a God of order, and everything that He does is done decently and in order. In the creation story, God used principles to bring order to the heavens and the earth. God created every creature and gave each a role, responsibility, and authority over a certain territory. This is the principle of jurisdiction. This is the model for most organizations and institutions, and it should be the model for us individually.

Many of the Biblical principles that we know well have long been practiced by many successful businesses and organizations. Corporations like Goldman Sachs, Walmart, and ExxonMobil, to name just a few, give away some portion of their profits to support other organizations or humanitarian efforts around the world. You may recognize this as tithing. Some of the most successful self-help, self-development, or growth programs in the world have forgiveness as a tenet. The Bible says in Matthew 7:12 NLT, "Do to others whatever you would like them to do to you. This is the essence of all that is taught in the law and the prophets." The secular world understands this as karma or the principle of cause-and-effect, where a person will experience what they do to others. We know this principle as reaping and sowing. We practice basic principles worldwide because principles work. In fact, principles are always at work whether or not we realize it. They are also at work whether we like it or not.

"Give, and it will be given to you. A good measure, pressed down, shaken together and running over, will be poured into your lap. For with the measure you use, it will be measured to you," (Luke 6:38 NIV).

If you are constantly judging and talking badly about others, it should not surprise you when others are doing the same to you. The principle of reaping and sowing is not just about money, it's about everything. It is worth taking the time to understand basic principles. For example, when things aren't going your way, and it seems that everything that can go wrong has gone wrong, we often skip over elementary principles and go straight to what my friend, Kimberly, and I call upper-division or PhD Jesus. That's where we just jump straight to trying to understand and explain God's will and His timing. We often don't even consider what we may have been *giving to others*, or what other basic principles we may have neglected and jump straight to discerning God's will and or His timing. This is like trying to solve a calculus problem without understanding basic math.

Sidebar: People often say that something is God's will and/or His timing when they don't have an answer to a difficult situation. Instead of this default answer, go back to the basics and determine if what you are doing, saying, and praying is in alignment with God's principles.

I submit to you that the old church had it right. As kids, we went to Sunday school to learn the basics. I loved Sunday school. My Sunday school teacher, Sis. Smith, was so sincere about trying to teach us kids the meaning of Noah's Ark, Jonah and the Whale, and countless other stories. As we got older, we were introduced to more complex ideas as we grew in Christ. I'm suggesting that we revisit the basic principles upon which our beliefs are rooted before we try to jump in at the graduate level. Some of us would do well just to sit with the simple idea that God is good all the time. I know we say it, but do we live our lives as though this were true?

You Can Count on Principles

I love principles because they provide predictability and consistency. Every time you throw an object into the air, you can predict that the object is going to come down. The atmospheric pressure and the density of the object may determine how quickly it comes down, but it will come down. Principles level the playing field. God never intended for some of His children to prosper and live an abundant life, while others could not. God left His principles for every one of us to use, and we experience their results based on how well we follow them.

In the natural world, it is certainly true that things are not always fair. Some of us were born into money and some into poverty. Some of us had two parents, and some were raised by grandparents or in foster homes. Some were handed everything they needed, and some had to work hard for everything they achieved.

As a judge, I know first-hand that the world is not always fair or just. Many of our society's laws exploit these inequalities by discriminating against the poor, the elderly, women, people of color, and every other marginalized group. However, when it comes to the higher laws like natural laws, and spiritual laws, we are all equal. It doesn't matter who throws an object into the air—a child, a rich woman, or a poor man—the object *will* consistently come back down. It doesn't matter who comes to Christ—an innocent child or a murderer—if they confess their sins and believe in Christ, they can freely receive the gift of salvation. Unlike people, governments, organizations, and institutions, principles do not discriminate. They cannot discriminate.

"For he [God] makes his sun rise on the evil and on the good, and sends rain on the just and on the unjust," (Matthew 5:45 ESV).

Why Do Bad Things Happen to Good People?

Principles are painfully consistent. Whether or not we believe in gravity, love gravity, or don't like it at all, it will be consistent. So many times, during a coaching or counseling session, I've heard, "I'm a good person. I read my Bible, pray, and go to church every week. Why doesn't this or that ever work out for me?"

I've said this myself, many times, about many different things. As a young lawyer, I was making more money than I ever had before. I was just happy to go from a starving student to a steady paycheck. But no matter how much money I made; my bank account stayed empty. A car repair, a busted water heater, and event after event kept robbing me of what should have been my *extra* money.

One day, I was driving home from work, and I was really complaining... I mean praying. *Why would you give me this job and keep me poor? I'm a good girl. I go to church. I pray. My very job is to help the indigent! I don't understand why you are doing this to me.*

I was really upset. I turned on the Christian radio station, and they were talking about tithing. Right there it hit me. Oops! I certainly was not tithing. I knew this principle because I had been a tither since Sunday school. At our church, the children received those little tithing cards. You put a dime in each of the little slots for each dollar you received during the week. On Sunday, you turned in the card for your Sunday school tithes offering. I remember tithing on my allowance and my birthday money for as long as I can remember. But I wasn't tithing during this time. I was just trying to catch up on a few bills and buy a few things that I wasn't able to afford as a law student. And, by the way, tithing on an attorney's salary was a lot different from adding dimes to a card. It sure seemed like a big check to write!

As soon as I realized I was neglecting the principle of tithing, I didn't even wait for Sunday. I went home and wrote a check for the appropriate amount and kept it in my Bible until Sunday. When it was time for the offering, I was the first one to stand, ready to drop my tithe in the offering basket. All I can tell you is that I have not suffered from lack in my finances ever since.

As I said, principles are painfully consistent. You cannot bargain or reason with them. Whether it's about forgiveness, treating others as you want to be treated, having integrity, or trying to figure out why you have no money—it is all regulated by principles. What you are experiencing is not personal, it's a principle.

God created principles to bring about order and predictability and to even out the playing field. That means that if you are not getting an expected result in a particular area, you may not be applying the proper principle, or you may not be applying any principle at all.

Principles Are More Important than Prayers.

I know that got your attention. Prayer is important, but if you're not in alignment with God's principles, your prayers will not be as effective. For example, the principle of seed, time, and harvest requires that you plant a seed in good ground, water it, and allow time for it to grow. Sometimes we are praying for things and we have not planted a seed. That would be like me standing on a pulpit and scattering seed and then praying over it. I can pray, fast, and prophesy over those seeds, but until I actually plant the seed in good ground, water it, and give it time to grow, I won't get the result I'm hoping for. Understand the principle before you begin to pray. I know that when I am frustrated with the results I'm getting, my first instinct may be to conclude that God wants me to pray more, fast more, give more, or wait longer. Or maybe it's just not His will or His timing that I should have what I'm praying for. However, I submit to you, that before you jump into an upper-division course and conclude what is God's will or His timing, do another thing, wait another day, another year, or even another decade, please consider that there may be a biblical principle you have overlooked. I am not saying you shouldn't exercise all the spiritual practices of praying, fasting, and/ or waiting. But what I am saying is that we often neglect the basic principles God left to lead and guide us. You may simply need to do your part to exercise the principle that governs the area you're praying about.

Miracles

"But what about miracles?" I can hear you ask. "Don't you believe in miracles?"

I absolutely believe in miracles. I am a beneficiary of God's miraculous power many times over. There are things that God has done that I could never do, create, or work out for myself, no matter what I did. When I was hoping to be appointed to a judgeship, everyone told me I needed to connect with someone on the *secret committee*— someone appointed by the governor to vet judicial hopefuls. Well, I had no connections with anyone in government or anyone on this committee. After all, it was the *secret* committee.

I was asked to attend a dinner to honor a friend. I said I would go, but when the date came, I was litigating a murder trial and I was exhausted. The dinner was in a neighboring city and the bay area traffic was in full effect. I started out in the direction of the event, but the traffic was so bad I realized I would never make it. So, I decided to turn back. Road construction forced everyone off of the freeway and onto the streets for a detour. Slowly, as I followed the cars winding through the streets, I realized the detour had taken me right where I needed to be. I parked and made it into the event right at the beginning.

As I mingled and chatted with the other guests, a co-worker introduced me to a man who seemed pleasant. When I finally made my way to my assigned seat, who was seated directly to my right? Yep, the person I was introduced to earlier. We talked about the event and about how I came to work at the Public Defender's office. I explained my desire to serve my community and how I thought my work could help me get justice for the indigent and other marginalized communities. Midway through dinner, my friend asked if I knew who I was seated next to. I said I had no idea, but we had been talking and he seemed very interested in my career and upbringing. It turns out that this man was the chair of this *secret committee!*

That's one in a million stories I can tell you about God's miraculous interventions. So yes, I believe in a God who allowed me to encounter a traffic jam to get me to a place I didn't want to go, to meet a person who would have a significant say in whether I was appointed to the bench. More times than I can count, God has opened doors I didn't know existed or orchestrated divine meetings for me with those who were instrumental in me getting certain jobs, assignments, or accolades, and even becoming a judge. God has created opportunities I could have never imagined or orchestrated for myself.

God, in His sovereignty, chose to set up the world using His principles and not miracles to govern it. But He can also choose to step outside of those principles and natural laws to do miraculous things for us. I know too many people who have been healed after doctors had given up on them to shrug off God's miraculous power. When God works a miracle, it is something that we could never do for ourselves. I don't ever recall a time in the New Testament where Jesus healed someone or performed some other miracle, like the feeding of the five thousand, where the people involved could possibly have accomplished that thing on their own. Hence, the term *supernatural* is used to describe times when God does more than what we can see or comprehend in the natural realm. When Jesus walked on water, He violated the law of Archimedes' Principle of Buoyancy. We also know that when Jesus raised Lazarus from the dead after three days, He violated every known natural and spiritual law. God is sovereign. In His sovereignty, He created principles and not miracles to govern our world. My philosophy is to practice the principles and keep your eyes open for miracles.

RECESS

Which biblical principles do you consistently practice?
What is the result?
Which principles have you ignored? What has resulted from this?
Recall a time when you observed or experienced a miracle.
(See Appendix C for a list of Biblical principles.)

CHAPTER 5

Discover How God Rules

Jesus Will *Not* Take the Wheel

Before we continue, we need to discover what part we have to play on this journey. God is sovereign. He has all power and all authority over all the universe. The universe has order because God presides. The sun rises and sets when it should, because God presides. Everything about the universe is precise and operates exactly the way it should, because God presides. And because God is sovereign, He could have used His unlimited power to reign and rule in any way that He chose. He could have chosen to rule humankind by creating us without free will, like robots who would do whatever He wanted. Instead, in His infinite wisdom, He designed us to make our own choices. He chose to rule by:

1) Leaving us instructions in His word. We have the option to follow His leadings and teachings or not.

2) In case we ever became confused and still didn't know what to do, God sent an example in the life of Jesus Christ.

3) And if that was not enough, God sent the Holy Spirit to empower us to do the things He has called us to do.

Because God has chosen to rule and reign in this way, this means that He has given us a part to play. We can follow His word, which instructs us to love or not love. We can be overly spiritual and confused and try to *divine* what God wants us to do, or we can simply follow His principles. We can live like many others and seek revenge or hold on to bitterness, or we can look to the example of Jesus and forgive. We can struggle with these things or allow the Holy Spirit to help and empower us whenever needed. In John 2:1-11, when Jesus does His first miracle by turning water into wine, the servants have a part to play. They were told to fill the pots with water. God made us stewards over the part He left for us to play.

God has given us authority over certain things and therefore we have a responsibility to steward those things. A steward is someone who is given authority to manage another's affairs. A steward is always given two things, authority and responsibility, and they are inextricably linked. A steward is duty-bound to do their part. This is why it is so important to know our part and how to do it effectively. I love singing the songs and hearing the messages that proclaim God can open doors and make ways out of no way. I believe He can because He is a sovereign God. That is the part that He has chosen to do. I love knowing that God can never fail in doing His part. However, if we don't do *our* part, it all falls apart. God can open doors and make ways, but if we don't walk through those doors and do something with

Sidebar: For just as the body without *the* spirit is dead, so also faith without works is dead. James 2:26 NASB

the ways He has made, what does it matter? An open door means nothing unless we do our part and walk through it. If we don't, we will remain stuck right where we are for months, years, and even decades.

When we don't do our part, we become spectators: those who only observe what is happening and can only beg God for a different outcome. A spectator is like a passenger in a car. She is along for the ride but has no power over when or by which route is used to get to the destination, or if she will reach the destination at all. She can see obstacles but can only voice opinions and pray that the driver heeds them. Spectators are merely observers and victims of whatever the driver does. Even if that means winding up in a ditch.

The good news is that God did not create us to be spectators. He created us to be stewards. As stewards, we are given the authority to drive our car (our lives) wherever we want to go. Yes, there are clear rules for driving our car, but God never intended for anyone else to drive your car but you. You get to decide how fast or slow to go, when to stop and re-fuel, or whether to go directly to your destination or take the scenic route. And even if you make a mistake and wind up in a ditch, you have the power to back up and go another way.

I know this may sound controversial to many who grew up hearing the phrase, "Jesus, take the wheel!" So many of us grew up hearing and believing that God would do everything for us—that He would micromanage our lives. That all we had to do was pray and God would do all the work and make sure we ended up exactly where He wanted us to be. We even sing songs about God being in control of every part of our lives. Not too long ago, I was in church and I was really enjoying our time of Praise and Worship. As the Praise and Worship team was singing, I heard the words, "And God will make all of my decisions for me." It jolted me out of my Praise and Worship experience. My eyes popped open, and I looked around to see if anyone else had heard what I thought I'd heard. They sang it again. "God will make all of my decisions for me." I know it is just a song, but it perfectly demonstrates how we may expect God to do what He's given us the authority to do.

Plainly put, God is not in control—at least not in the way most of us believe He is. God is sovereign, but He chose to give us authority over our own lives. He will not make our decisions for us or do the things He has given us the authority to do. He gave us a part to play in our own lives. Yes, we commune with Him daily to know the route we should take, but Jesus will not take the wheel. God has given us everything we need to drive our own car. He's given us the direction, lighting, and fuel. Folks, He even gave us the car! The direction, speed, and route you choose to drive are up to you. This may be a little nuanced from what we normally hear in church, but hang in there with me. I promise I'm still in the Book. The bottom line is that God is king, and he sits on the throne and presides over the universe and everything in it. However, He has chosen to give us a part to play, and that is to preside over everything He has given to us. Are you doing your part?

RECESS

Are you waiting for God to take the wheel in some area of your life?
Is it an area where God has left an instruction for you to take the wheel?
What steps can you take to get back into the driver's seat in this area?

Everybody Has a Part

People often ask me what it was like to be a judge. It is extremely empowering. The best way to describe what I did is that I brought order to chaos. Think about it. The only time we find ourselves in court is when something is out of order. It could be something in your personal life, with society, an organization, or even the government. No matter what the situation, when things are out of order, it requires a higher authority to re-establish order.

Basically, a judge is a steward. I did not own my department, but the Governor of the State of California made me a steward over it. That means the State had delegated to me certain authority to do a specific job. If you fell under my jurisdiction, I had been given the authority to tell people what they could and could not do. My orders were not suggestions, and they had to be followed, or there would be consequences. If you fell under my jurisdiction, I could order money to be taken from one person and given to another. I could order who you could or could not associate with. I could order what time you had to be home at night or where you could go during the day. I could order on what dates and times you could see your children and where you could or could not reside. I could even tell people, in certain situations, what color clothing they could wear. One of the greatest powers I could wield was to put someone in or release them from jail. These are serious powers invested in the office of a judge. But with that authority comes a great responsibility. I couldn't just do whatever I wanted. I had to

Sidebar: There were many happy times when I could perform marriages or adoptions, but mostly, people come to court when things are out of order.

ensure that my rulings adhered to the law and that my orders were not arbitrary or capricious but just and fair.

I was entrusted with this awesome authority because I answered the call, had taken an oath, and had sworn an oath to carry out my duty according to the law. The only reason that our judicial system works is because every participant knows and does their part. In a courtroom, everybody submits to the jurisdiction or authority of the judge. Everybody not only knows their part, but they are sworn to do their part. Once they take an oath, they become stewards of the process. Each player has a different part and everyone is duty-bound to play that part. An attorney's job as an advocate is to try to influence the judge and the jury on their theory of the case. Every lawyer takes an oath to do so within the bounds of the law. Before a witness can offer evidence, they must swear an oath to tell the truth. Even jurors are sworn to follow certain guidelines when determining guilt or innocence.

My job, as the judge, was to preside. That is:

- to ensure that things were fair and just,
- to ensure that only those with standing were allowed to participate in the process,
- to make sure there was a good record by ensuring that only competent and admissible evidence came into the hearing,
- to strike things from the record that shouldn't be there.

My job was to make the tough decisions and exercise authority where I should, and never exert my authority where I should not. The bottom line was to make sure that there was order, and that there was a proper outcome according to the law.

While it can be daunting to be responsible for proceedings that can affect so many lives, I took comfort in the fact that, wherever I have been given responsibility, I have been given authority. That meant that if I didn't like the way things were going in my courtroom, I could change it. Since I didn't have authority over anything outside of my courtroom, I was not responsible for it.

There was one occasion when I was sitting in a criminal assignment. My job was to do felony arraignments. That means I determined who should be held in custody or released pending their next hearing. These were difficult and sometimes heart-wrenching decisions that I had to make based on the facts, regardless of how I felt about the individual case. This required me to make very serious and complex decisions in a very short amount of time, often with very little information.

Whenever I released someone from custody, I always said the same thing. "Sir/Madam, I am releasing you from custody. Please obey all laws and make all of your court appearances, and stay in touch with your lawyer. Please do your part."

What I was really saying here is that someone has alleged that you have not done your part as a citizen, either by taking something that does not belong to you, endangering, hurting, or injuring someone, or breaking some other law. I'm going to release you, but I need you to do your part as a good citizen. I need you to steward yourself. If you cannot steward or manage yourself, I will have you placed back in custody so that the system can manage you.

If they knew their role and played their part as a responsible citizen, then it was likely I wouldn't see them again. However, if they didn't play their part, perhaps by disobeying another law, failing to make their court appearance, or disobeying some other order I've given, I would soon see them back in my court again.

Sidebar: Our criminal justice system is complex and plagued with systemic injustice for many. There are many reasons for this, including the struggle with housing and other basic needs, mental health issues, abuse, addiction, and other serious concerns that hinder people from doing their part. I'm simplifying this complex issue to highlight those who can but choose not to do their part.

I could always discern within a matter of seconds who had played their part and who had not. When I asked someone if they had done what they were supposed to do, those who did simply said yes or smiled. Those who hadn't usually offered excuses or blamed some other person, entity, or circumstance.

"Sir/ma'am, did you do what I ordered you to do?"

"Well, what had happened was..." and then I would hear a laundry list of excuses.

When you don't do your part, you are out of order. Sadly, this can lead to confinement and/or restriction. Not just for those who appear before me, but for all of us. If you find yourself stuck, experiencing lack, or unable to move forward in some area of your life, you should ask yourself, am I doing my part? Am I out of order?

RECESS

Is there an area of your life where you feel stuck?

Are you out of order because you are not doing your part?

Are you doing your part to exercise your authority over that area?

To help with this exercise, download a copy of the Do Your Part

Worksheet by going to: shelynabrown.com/preside-thebookworksheets

CHAPTER 6

The Oath

Every journey requires a commitment. Nearly all service professionals take an oath. Those in the military and those who hold public office, including the President of the United States, take an oath. An oath is a solemn promise that you will submit to the proper authority and carry out your duties and responsibilities in a dignified way. An oath is an outward or public affirmation of the call to stewardship. An oath simply states that you will be a good steward over whatever you are being given to manage.

My commitment to becoming a judge was more than "I really enjoy the law." The oath was an affirmative commitment and a declaration that I was willing to submit all of my personal and political opinions, attitudes, and feelings, to judge all persons who come before me fairly, according to the laws of California and the County of Santa Clara. This is the oath I took:

I, Shelyna V Brown, do solemnly swear (or affirm) that I will support and defend the Constitution of the United States and the Constitution of the State of California against all enemies, foreign and domestic; that I will bear true faith and allegiance to the Constitution of the United States and the State of California; that I take this obligation freely, without any mental reservation or purpose of evasion; and that I will well and faithfully discharge the duties upon which I am about to enter, and during such time as I hold the office of Superior court judge.

In taking the oath, I agreed that in carrying out my duty, I would submit to and exercise the authority given to me by the state. I pledged that I would live my life according to the code of judicial ethics and not bring shame or reproach upon the office. It was a very sobering moment. I remember standing there with my right hand raised. My heart was pounding as I recited the words. I had memorized the oath, so I was concentrating on not speaking the words before the judge who was administering the oath. After I recited the oath, I remember hearing some claps and some shouts of, "Yes!" and "Woo!" All I could think at that moment was, *I'm really a judge. This is amazing!*

Taking the oath is akin to accepting Christ. The oath is not just saying that I accept Jesus just as my savior, but I submit to His authority as Lord. You are taking an oath to be a steward of everything God has given you to manage. It means that you will submit to and exercise the authority He has given to you. While God has given you authority to sit on the bench and preside over your life, only the King of Kings sits on the throne. This means that all of your authority derives from Him and you must submit who you are to His will and His ways. Just like a judge becomes a steward of her courtroom, you become a steward of your life. No one has the authority to manage my courtroom but me.

No one has the authority to manage your life but you. God gives you the authority, and He does not come down and micromanage your life. He left principles and instructions and gave us roles, responsibilities, and boundaries to help us be good stewards.

Once you have taken the oath, you do not just have permission, but you have a duty, a mandate to preside over or manage all the issues that come into your jurisdiction. It means you are responsible for everything that happens in your jurisdiction. Not everything may be your fault, but everything is your responsibility. An oath is not something to be taken lightly.

Before I took my oath, I spent several days reflecting on the momentous task I was about to undertake. I thought about what I was really pledging with that oath. Did I really believe I could do all I was called to do? How would a little girl from the west side of Fresno be able to do such a big job? I began to have doubts and became fearful. Then I remembered that someone prayed over me with the prayer that King Solomon prayed in 2 Chronicles 1:1 (NKJV), "Now give me wisdom and knowledge, that I may go out and come in before this people; for who can judge this great people of Yours?" When it was all said and done, I had to go back to my beliefs. If God called me to do this, then He would equip me. I had to believe that God was good and not setting me up to fail.

God has given you everything you need to be a good steward of your life. When in doubt, pray and ask God to guide you.

RECESS

Have you made the commitment to be a good steward?

If you haven't taken the oath, turn to Appendix A and take the oath. Share your experience with a friend.

CHAPTER 7

The Robe

When you become a judge, part of the ceremony involves being given a new garment. I am so grateful that both my mother and father were present to robe me. They were so proud as they walked up the stairs of that stage to join me. My mom and dad were smiling as they approached me. I could see tears in my dad's eyes. As I handed them the robe, I couldn't help but be grateful that I had such amazing parents. I was delighted they could see this day. This was just as much their achievement as it was mine. They stood on either side of me, each helping to put my right and then my left arm into the robe and then settling it on my shoulders. My mom couldn't help but smooth out the robe and make sure it was straight. This moment was symbolic of how my parents had been by my side through every other difficult and joyous time of my life.

I get teary even thinking about how much they sacrificed so that I could wear that robe. My family had *In honor of MLB*, my paternal grandmother's initials, Minnie Lee Brown, sewn into my robe next to my initials. It is so fitting because she walked me through my first and most important call and oath. Every time I put on that robe, I am reminded that I stand on the shoulders of everyone who came before me. I live the dream they didn't have the opportunity to live.

The robe symbolizes the fact that you do not represent yourself when you step into the courtroom. You represent the government of the United States. The robe covers all my inadequacies and insecurities. It symbolizes something greater than me. Whoever dons the robe is given the honor and respect that the position, not the person, demands. The robe reminds you and those in the courtroom of your authority and your responsibility to preside over the proceedings.

As it is with the judicial robe, we get a robe of righteousness when we answer the call and take the oath to follow Christ. You are then clothed with the garment of salvation and covered with the robe of righteousness. Unlike a judicial robe, the robe of righteousness is freely given, not earned. This robe is not to be removed and represents God's cover and protection.

"I delight greatly in the LORD; my soul rejoices in my God. For he has clothed me with garments of salvation and arrayed me in a robe of his righteousness, as a bridegroom adorns his head like a priest, and as a bride adorns herself with her jewels," (Isaiah 61:10 NIV).

The robe reminds us that it is no longer all about us. We now represent something greater than ourselves. Every day, you must remember to take off your old self and accept that God has made you righteous. You've done nothing to earn it. This robe is a gift from God.

RECESS

What does the robe of righteousness mean to you?
Are you trying to earn the robe of righteousness?

CHAPTER 8

Stewardship and the Parable
of the Ten Talents

Discover the Parable

The Parable of the Ten Talents is where we get our understanding of the principle of stewardship. Stewardship is often an overlooked biblical principle, but as I began to study it, I realized it had powerful implications for my life. It is the basis of most governmental and societal structures. It is the basis on which I had invested authority as a judge, and it is the basis of the authority God has given me to be a good steward of my life. After God created man and woman in His own image, He gave the command to be fruitful and multiply. We are to use everything at our disposal to preside, that is, to grow, mature, and be fruitful in every area that we are called to manage. As we will see in the Parable of the Ten Talents, being fruitful not only benefits us greatly, it glorifies God. We also learn from the parable that when we are good stewards, we are blessed with even more to manage. From our abundance, we can bless others.

A parable is simply a story that teaches a lesson. On the surface, the lesson is usually very straightforward and practical. However,

Sidebar: In my discussion of the Parable of the Ten Talents, (Matthew 25:14–30 ESV), I will use the pronoun *she* when referring to the servant's actions, reflecting how I see myself in scripture, although the scripture uses *he*.

there is usually a deeper moral or spiritual lesson hidden in the story. The Parable of the Ten Talents teaches the simple and practical lesson of managing your money or other resources. Upon closer inspection, we can see that while this parable teaches the principle of stewardship, it is not just about money and tangible resources, but of being a steward over everything we are, and have been, given by God.

Ownership versus Stewardship

"For it will be like a man going on a journey, who called his servants and entrusted to them his property. To one he gave five talents, to another two, to another one, to each according to his ability. Then he went away" (Matthew 25:14-15, ESV).

We can see that the man, or master as he is referred to in other translations, was the owner. He left the talents in the servants' care. Any discussion of stewardship must begin here. The servants did not own anything, but they were left in charge of it. We know that we did not create ourselves, but it was God who created us. We cannot own what we did not create, but we are responsible to steward what God left to us.

"He who had received the five talents went at once and traded with them, and he made five talents more. So also, he who had the two talents made two talents more. But he who had received one talent went and dug in the ground and his his master's money" (Matthew 25:16-18, ESV).

Sidebar: One talent = $400,000.00 or close in American dollars today, so even one talent is a lot!

Responsibility

Each individual was given a role, responsibility, and authority for what they had been given. Two servants went out and traded immediately. One servant hid what she had been given in a hole. The master did not micromanage their activity or non-activity.

"Now after a long time the master of those servants came and settled accounts with them" (Matthew 25:19, ESV).

Accountability

Every servant was accountable for what she had been given.

"And he who had received the five talents came forward, bringing five talents more, saying, 'Master, you delivered to me five talents; here, I have made five talents more.' His Master said to him, 'Well done, good and faithful servant. You have been faithful over a little; I will set you over much. Enter into the joy of your master.' And he also who had the two talents came forward, saying, 'Master, you delivered to me two talents; here, I have made two talents more." His Master said to him, 'Well done, good and faithful servant. You have been faithful over a little; I will set you over much. Enter into the joy of your master'" (Matthew 25:20-23, ESV).

Reward/Consequences

The two servants who properly stewarded what they were given were fruitful. As a reward, they were given even more resources to steward. They were also invited to celebrate with the master.

"He also who had received the one talent came forward, saying, 'Master, I knew you to be a hard man, reaping where you did not sow, and gathering where you scattered no seed, so I was afraid, and I went and hid your talent in the ground. Here, you have what is yours.' But his master answered him, 'You wicked and slothful servant! You knew that I reap where I have not sown and gather where I scattered no seed? Then you ought to have invested my money with the bankers, and at my coming I should have received what was my own with interest. So take the talent from him and give it to him who has the ten talents. For to everyone who has will more be given, and he will have an abundance. But from the one who has not, even what he has will be taken away. And cast the worthless servant into the outer darkness. In that place there will be weeping and gnashing of teeth'" (Matthew 25:24-30, ESV).

Consequence

The one who was too afraid to steward had to face the consequences of her inaction. She was deemed wicked and slothful and what she had was taken away. The consequence of failing to steward what you have been given is lack. The reward for being a good steward is fruitfulness, receiving more than what you started with. I love the quote by Bob Goff. "You don't always get to pick the parable we're living, but we get to pick who we are in the parable." I choose to be a good steward. Who will you choose to be?

The Four Tenets

The parable of the Ten Talents beautifully demonstrates four tenets that impact one's ability to be a good steward:

1) How you see God,
2) How you see yourself,
3) Ability/Willingness to follow instructions, and
4) Exercising an affirmative duty to do your part.

First Tenet—How You See God

In this parable, each of the servants was given an opportunity, and each opportunity was commensurate with their ability. How they responded to the opportunity was first based on what they believed about the Master. In verses 24-25, we see what the servant believed about the Master. She believed the Master to be a hard, unfair, and unreasonable man. For this reason, she was afraid to trade or make a mistake, so she hid what she had in the ground. She did not believe that the master was good. Where did she get this paralyzing belief? Was it true? Was it reasonable? Remember, beliefs can be powerful or paralyzing, but they don't have to be true.

Often, we don't do what we know to do because, like this servant, we are afraid of making a mistake. We wrap it in spiritual language and hide behind phrases like:

- *I'm praying on it.*
- *I'm just waiting on the Lord.*
- *I'm waiting on a sign.*
- *If it's His will, it will happen.*
- *I don't want to be out of God's will/timing.*

This is what I said initially about becoming a judge. The truth was, I was afraid that my dream was too big and that I would fail, and it kept me paralyzed for months. If I had never done my part, God's will for me would have never come to pass. Does this sound like anything you've heard or even said lately? What is it that makes us believe anything we do or don't do could hamper God's plans, or be outside of the timing or will of an omnipotent God who knows our *end* from the *beginning*? Even if it were possible to miss God, God cannot miss us. What we're really afraid of is punishment for making a mistake. Ask yourself, if I believe God is truly a good God, a merciful and loving God, what am I really afraid of? Even if I make a mistake, how would a good, loving, and merciful God respond? How you move through the world, and what you choose to do and not do is, first and foremost, based on whether or not you truly believe God is good or whether you believe He is waiting for you to make a mistake so He can punish you. My girlfriend calls this Clipboard God. As a child, she had an image of God walking around with a clipboard, just waiting to write down when you made a mistake. Didn't say evening prayers? Check! Didn't read your Bible today? Check! For many, this childhood image is how many feel about a God they describe as good.

Did the other servants share this belief about the master? I don't believe they did because they went out and traded. They took action, not knowing what the outcome would be. But even if they did share this belief, they still went out and traded, even if they were afraid. Doing things afraid is a lesson I've had to learn over the years. I have done things that I have been truly afraid would fail, such as becoming a judge or even writing this book. But I'm no longer afraid that I will lose the love of God or be punished for being outside of His will.

When I failed at becoming a judge the first time, I was upset with God because that part of the journey was not my idea. But for a prophetic word and a nudge from a judge I respected, I would never have tried to become a judge. I admit, when I first realized I had not been selected to be a judge, I immediately thought I was being punished for being outside of God's will or timing, or just reaching too high. But then I realized that mistakes, failures, and missteps are just a part of life. After a three-month pity party, I dusted myself off and tried again. The second time I applied, the process went so smoothly and quickly that I forgot all about the failure. I'll also note that the year I did not get the judgeship, seven judges from my county were appointed. The following year, I was the *only* judge appointed in my county, and I received all kinds of special attention and treatment. When you do your part, God is always faithful to do His part.

RECESS

In which areas of your life are you using the bullet-
pointed phrases above?
Are you often afraid to make decisions because you believe
God is waiting to punish you?
Name an area where you have been waiting on God but have not done
your part. What are you waiting for?
Name the ways in which God has been good to you recently.
Do you believe God is punishing you by withholding
good things from you?

Second Tenet—How You See Yourself

The second tenet that can drastically affect what kind of steward you are is how you see yourself. Two of the servants believed they had what they needed to do the job they were called to do. If you think about it, why would the master choose someone who was incapable of making a return on his/her investment? If you believe the master set the third servant up to fail so he could deliver a punishment, I would invite you to go back to the previous section and ask yourself if this is what a good and loving God would do.

At first blush, this may look like the Master was playing favorites by giving each servant a different number of talents. However, God created us, and He knows exactly what we can handle. Everything God has given us is a gift. All of our spiritual gifts and natural talents come from God. Some of us can sing, paint, organize, or have an innate ability to connect with people. There are so many gifts I could not possibly begin to list them. But a gift is usually that thing you do that people marvel at, yet it comes so easily to you. It's that thing that you know you do well, but you don't know why, or how you do it well. You just can. Some of the things we take for granted, like being able to speak a kind word or a word of encouragement at just the right time, are gifts.

In addition to all of those wonderful gifts, God has also given us the ability to think, emote, and experience the world around us. He has also given us the ability to reason and make decisions. All of these things are ours to steward. We are all unique and there is no one like you on the planet. Someone may look like you or have similar skills and gifts, but no one can do *exactly* what you can do, the way you can do it. God knew that and gave you exactly what you need to fulfill your specific purpose. It is an act of grace and mercy that God does not give us more than we can handle.

The fact is, the master chose each servant because He believed she was capable of doing the job. The problem was, the servant didn't believe it. The same goes for you and me. The only reason we are here is because God believed we were worthy of life. And not just any old life, but an abundant and fruitful life. God would not have given you your life if he didn't believe that you were capable of stewarding it. Whatever you have right now is enough to accomplish what you were put here on this earth to accomplish. God would not have entrusted your life—your body, your spirit, your soul—to you if he did not trust that you are able to manage it. If you are here, you have enough. You ARE enough. You are worthy of your life, not because of anything you have done, but because God said so. What are you going to do with what you have?

Recess

Do you feel if you prayed, studied your Bible more, or were a better Christian, God would be more pleased with you and bless you more? Do you ever feel guilty about your blessings and try to explain or justify why you're worthy of God's blessings?
What dreams or desires have you buried in a hole?

Third Tenet—Following Instructions/Implementing Principles

When the master left, there was no mention of him pulling either of the servants aside to give them any special instructions or tools. He just left them to do what they were supposed to do. He did not come back to check on their progress or micromanage them along the way. The two servants who received the five talents and two talents, respectively, went at once and began to trade. They didn't ask questions or contemplate whether they were able. Dare I say, they didn't even pray about it. They just went and did what they knew to do.

How did the two servants know what to do? Did the master favor them more and give them a secret manual or set of instructions? Sometimes we see people who have something or are doing something that we want to have or do. Immediately, we think they have something we don't have: favor, money, a parent in the business, or some other special skill or talent. Often, they are just exercising the principle or following the instruction that is available to all of us. I believe the servants had observed the master and other servants over the years and saw what they had done. Maybe the servants sought wise counsel from others who had taken care of the master's business before them. Whatever they did, they discovered what they needed to know, and more importantly, two of them had the courage to act on it immediately. God wants you to be fruitful. As the steward of your life, you are the only one who can go out and accomplish that. Will you go out at once, or are you still praying about it?

Fourth Tenet—Affirmative Duty to Act/Steward

I want to be clear that I am not suggesting that we should not pray for God's direction or wait for God's timing. I believe in the power of prayer. When we pray, we are in fellowship with God. In prayer, if we are quiet and allow Him to, He reveals ideas, plans, and strategies and brings comfort. I could talk all day about the benefits of prayer, but that is a different book. However, I believe that there are times when we use prayer as an excuse not to do what we know we should do. I know I have. Years ago, I was praying about ending a romantic relationship. The answer was very clear. Shelyna, this is not the relationship for you. But for many reasons, including the fact that I was in my forties and I really wanted to get married, I didn't want to do what I knew I should do. So, I kept praying about it. The answer never changed, but I prayed about it for months. My delay caused a great deal of pain that could have been avoided had I heeded the call months earlier.

We have a tendency to put off things that are difficult or will cause ourselves or others pain. Has there ever been a time when you prayed about something you already knew the answer to? Are you praying about something now and you already know the answer, but you don't want to do it? Maybe you know that by heeding the answer, you will experience pain or that you will cause someone else pain. Maybe you do not want to make the decision because it will make you appear selfish, mean to others, or hurt someone's feelings. When I presided as a judge, I made unpopular rulings every day. In fact, one of my mentors told me that I would know I'd done my job if both sides were at least a little unhappy with my rulings. I didn't do it to be mean or hurtful, but I had an affirmative duty to do the right thing, no matter how I or anybody else felt about it.

I should also tell you that there are some things we don't even have to pray about. Shocking, right? Sure, you may want to pray about timing and/or strategy, but if there is a clear principle, you should do it without delay. If there is a friend or a job that is asking you to cheat or be dishonest, you don't really have to pray about that, do you? When you know you should apologize or forgive someone, we know what God's answer is going to be, don't we? We know what God's word says about kindness and forgiveness, don't we? There was a situation where I knew I owed my colleague an apology, but I spent two days praying about it despite knowing immediately what I needed to do. But I didn't want to do it because I was ashamed of my behavior. I was worried about how they would respond, so I delayed my apology. Is there something you've been praying about for weeks, months, or even years? We often spiritualize things when what we need to do is make a decision to follow the principle. Never underestimate the power of a decision. I understand that forgiving some things is harder than others. For example, forgiving someone for betraying your trust is harder than forgiving someone for being late or not returning your call. In fact, forgiving some things or people may be a lengthy process. However, the *decision* that you will forgive should come quickly. The servants who went out immediately to trade made a decision to do so. Is there a decision that you need to make? If you're not sure, think about what you've been praying about for a while. Check to see if you're experiencing lack in that area. I guarantee that wherever you're experiencing lack, it's a place that needs to be stewarded properly.

RECESS

Have you been waiting and praying about a situation for a while?
Has God left an instruction or a principle for you to follow?
If you have not followed it, why not?

You Have Backup

Two of the servants went out and doubled what they had been given to manage. What did it take to trade? They first had to leave the comfort of their home and go out to where business was being conducted. People during this time often carried a seal or other object to let people know they had their master's authority to trade on his behalf. I believe they had a seal or token proving they had their master's authority to trade on his behalf. Remember, everything we do is on behalf of the master.

When I sat on the bench, I could have been nervous and quite intimidated about making such momentous decisions, if I were making all those tough decisions in my own name and from my own thoughts and feelings. But I was not acting on my own. I was a steward. I was acting on behalf of the State of California. I had to do my part and study the law and make sure that I understood the proper procedures and protocols. Knowing that I was acting on behalf of the State of California helped me to feel bold and confident. Not because of me, but because of who I represented. Just like those servants, I was a steward, and when I was acting within my jurisdiction on behalf of the government, I had great confidence. After all, I had the full authority of the State of California behind me.

When you receive something that you are to steward, begin immediately. Sometimes, beginning immediately may involve gathering more information, finding out the principle or the applicable instruction, consulting with others, or assessing the right time to begin. But it is not waiting for a sign of whether or not to steward. When I sat in my capacity as a judge, I consulted the statutes, sought more information from the attorneys, or sought wise counsel from my colleagues. But I never asked permission to do what I had been given authority to do. I presided. The two servants in the parable didn't ask permission to be fruitful. They simply did what needed to be done. They did their part. They exercised their authority as stewards. What have you been given authority to do?

What Is Wrong with the Status Quo?

On the face of it, it doesn't seem so bad for the one servant simply to return to the master what she was given. After all, she didn't return *less* than what she received. I used to think that maybe the master overreacted. However, if the only point of receiving the talents was to multiply them, then I understand why the master was upset. The servant's job was to increase and progress, just as we are to be fruitful and multiply. The master points out in verse 27 that even putting the money in a bank where it could earn interest would be far better than hiding it. That one servant wasn't given a different set of instructions or treated differently in some way. She was given the same opportunity as the other servants.

What made her experience different from the others? It was her beliefs about the master. She believed he was a hard man. But it was also her beliefs about herself. She believed she was not capable or worthy of going out to trade. It was either her inability or unwillingness to implement the instructions, and she failed to act. Instead of stewarding what she had been given, she became a spectator, waiting to see what would happen. As a result, she experienced lack when the other servants were fruitful.

RECESS

Is there any area in your life where you have not seen an increase for years or decades? What can you do to begin to steward that area?

CHAPTER 9

Mindset Awareness

The Mindset for the Journey

When I was first appointed to the bench, I had no idea how much emphasis was placed on the judge's robe. I received several unsolicited emails from sitting judges opining about the best type of robe. *Definitely get the snaps. No, a zipper is best. Get the full sleeves. No, the sleeves should be tailored. A robe should have piping on the collar. No piping, too ostentatious.* Honestly, I thought every robe was exactly the same. I found out that there are as many different robes as there are judges. However, the robe is unifying because it symbolizes who you must become when you put it on.

Donning the robe is like putting on a mindset. It is something every judge must do before they can preside. Every judge may approach things differently, but we all have the mindset that we are stewards, responsible for ensuring the right outcome. No judge would even consider going out to the bench to preside without the robe. In fact, it is a misdemeanor to do so. The robe was a reminder that I was not ruling or presiding as Shelyna, but as Judge Brown. I was the steward of this department. Shelyna has beliefs and biases and insecurities that might not have allowed me to do my job as a fair and impartial arbiter of the law and the facts. When I put on that robe, I was fully aware of my beliefs, biases, and imperfections. However, they were no longer relevant. What was relevant was doing what was fair and just under the law. Putting on the robe meant I had stepped into the role of steward over this department. I fully embraced my role and did my best to do my part. The robe is also a beautiful metaphor for how we can and must adopt the mindset of a steward over that of a spectator. Every time I donned my robe, I put on the mindset of a judge and steward.

Everything begins with awareness. You can't assess, modify, or change anything unless you are aware of it. Many people are not aware that they even have a particular mindset. A mindset is simply a set of beliefs and attitudes that shape how you make sense of the world. It influences how you think, feel, and behave in any given situation. Some mindsets are empowering and some are disempowering.

A mindset is like a filter through which we interpret information and our experiences. Seeing life through rose-colored glasses is an idiom that represents the idea that two people can receive the same information or experience the same thing, but the person with the rose-colored glasses will interpret that information or experience with a more positive or rosy outlook. For example, one mindset might see the end of a relationship or a job loss as the end of the world, while another might see it as an opportunity for a change for the better. Two people can experience the same thing, even something as devastating as abuse or trauma, and have two different takeaways from the experience. Their mindset will determine how they will respond to that experience.

One of the hardest parts of my job was sentencing a person when they had been convicted or pled guilty to a crime. Often the victims of the crime will want to be heard before I sentence a person. I'll never forget a young girl of only fourteen who stood before me to deliver a statement before I rendered a sentence in a child sexual assault case. The defendant had been found guilty of abusing her. She told me that, while she had been victimized, she was not a victim. She said that she was in counseling and struggling to make sense of things. She told me she would get her revenge by living a good life and being successful, despite what this person had done to her. I still think about how determined she was to steward her future and not just wait and watch life happen to her. She was determined not to be defined by one traumatic experience. I don't know what happened to her, but I know she had a fighting chance because she believed that she, not her circumstance, would decide who and what she could become.

We may have different mindsets for different areas of our lives. For example, you may have an empowering mindset about your finances. That is, for the most part, you believe you have control over your spending and saving. You believe that you have the power to improve your finances, if necessary. However, you may have a disempowering mindset about your health. That is, you believe there is absolutely nothing you can do to improve your health—that your health is something you cannot steward. Maybe because of a statistic that you saw, or you believe something to be hereditary, and therefore outside of your ability to steward.

"My grandmother told me that all the women in my family are overweight. We have always been overweight and you are gonna be overweight. So, I just always thought I would be the same. That's just the way it is."

This is what someone said to me about their health and body image. This is someone who, since childhood, believed she had no control over their health or body image.

This is not a discussion about weight but about having a disempowering mindset about one's own health. Because my friend did not believe she could steward her weight, she never really tried, and when she did, she did so half-heartedly. She didn't really think any health or fitness plan would work because *it runs in the family*. I submit that it may not be that it runs in the family so much as the diet, habits, and/or lifestyle runs in the family. So many of my family and friends have the following disempowering mindsets about health and other areas of our lives:

- If my mother had high blood pressure and/or diabetes, I know I will have it too.
- My father was an alcoholic. I am doomed to become an alcoholic.
- All the women in my family are single mothers. Therefore, I will end up as a single mother, too.
- No one in my family has gone to college. I will not be able to go to college either.

The list of what we do not steward because we believe we have no power to do so is endless. I have heard these cycles referred to as familial or generational curses. I have observed certain families that have three to four generations in the court system. Was everyone with this last name cursed to a life of criminality? The reality is, if you dig a hole like the servant in the parable, and do not even try to steward an area, you will experience lack. If you can disrupt the belief, you can break the cycle. I have a friend who grew up in foster homes. She was told not to think about college and just get a job. Any job. She was told that nobody in her family had ever gone to college or even moved out of their small town and she wouldn't either. My friend decided she wanted more than what she had seen those around her become and more than what she was told she could become. She rejected what she had been told and even what she was experiencing and began to steward this area of her life. When I met her in college, she was the most dedicated and determined person I had ever met. She is now a professional with a master's degree, living a beautiful life. What would happen if we stewarded these areas we had previously written off as being hereditary or predetermined? The importance of the proper mindset cannot be overstated. The Bible is clear. Whatever we steward becomes fruitful. Whatever we put in a hole, or fail to steward, yields lack. If there is any area of your life that you want to change, even those areas where those before you and those around you suffered lack, you can break the cycle, but you must first change your mindset.

RECESS

Are you aware of your mindsets?
Which areas of your life do you feel confident to steward?
Which areas do you feel are out of your ability to steward?
What generational curses have you been told plague your family?
How can you steward for a better outcome?

Two Mindsets—Steward or Spectator?

As Christians, we all believe in the basic tenets of our faith. We believe God is sovereign. We believe the Bible to be the infallible word of God. We believe Christ died for our sins. It is how people interpret what these things mean that has created the many denominations within the Christian faith. Our mindsets or our filters determine how we will perceive these tenets and how we will respond to them.

There are two mindsets I like to focus on: that of Steward and Spectator. I point them out because one produces fruitfulness and one produces lack. This does not mean one makes you a good person and the other makes you a bad person. Instead, one is empowering and produces a feeling of agency, while the other is disempowering and produces a feeling of helplessness or victimhood. We all embody each of these mindsets in one area of our lives or another. If we had the choice, wouldn't it be nice to embrace the mindset that produces fruitfulness instead of lack?

I have spent nearly thirty years counseling people in diverse arenas. As a public defender, I counseled criminal defendants and their families on how to defend their criminal cases. As a mentor and life coach, I have supported people as they take on new challenges in life. As a minister, I have had the privilege to pray with, care for, and support people who were going through some of the most difficult times of their lives. As a judge, I listened to some of the most horrendous and heartbreaking stories. I not only heard from those accused of committing crimes, but also from the victims of those crimes. I heard from family members and advocates on both sides of the story.

No matter what the arena, I have found one thing to be true: two major mindsets are at work—the *Steward* or the *Spectator*. The *Steward*, like the judge who presides over all that they have been given, believes they are responsible for their decisions. If they are not, then who is? Whereas *Spectators* often believe they have no control over what is happening to them, and that it is other people or circumstances or even God or the Devil that are making them do or keeping them from doing something.

Again, we all have been both stewards and spectators in different areas throughout our lives. Many of you reading this book may be very accomplished in your career and finances. Others may have flourishing relationships with family and friends, and others are experiencing consistent spiritual growth. We can feel empowered and fruitful in some areas of our lives and at the same time, overwhelmed by fear, doubt, or depression in other areas. This makes us human. The key is to identify where we are spectators and begin the journey to becoming stewards over every area of our lives.

The Stewardship Mindset

A Stewardship Mindset is what one must have in order to preside. It is a mindset that understands you have permission and the duty to steward your own life. Think of your life as a car. The driver of the car is a steward. The passenger is just a spectator. The steward does not just have permission to drive the car, but a responsibility to do so once they get behind the wheel.

When I became a judge, I continued to mentor students and young lawyers. People had always sought me out for advice or guidance, but when I became a judge, that number seemed to skyrocket! I decided to get a certificate in coaching from the iPEC (Institute for Professional Excellence in Coaching) so I could better support people. The tools I gained have come in handy in ministry and on the bench. I remember in one of the first classes the instructor said we can't live the life we want until we decide to do so. They went on to say that we were living the life we had chosen to live, but we could create a different, better life at any time. I don't know why but felt uncomfortable with this idea.

At the same time, this also resonated with me. I wanted to be a lawyer and then a judge, and I was able to accomplish those things because I decided to do so. However, if I was experiencing lack or some difficult place, wasn't that just my cross to bear or the season that I had to endure? Was I a bad Christian to even think I could choose what I wanted to do, be, or have? Wasn't that God's job? I had just been appointed to the bench; I was in a promising relationship;

and I was healthy. What if wanting more was just greedy? Shouldn't I just be content with what I had? What if what I wanted differed from what God wanted for me? My mind was racing. This one session challenged me to think about what I had always believed about God and His will for my life.

I'm always open to new ideas and concepts, but if they contradict God's words or His principles, I cannot embrace them. I selected this particular coaching program because I recognized all of their foundational principles as biblical principles; believing in a power higher than yourself, loving and forgiving others, prayer and meditation, treating others as you want to be treated, and tithing, to name a few.

Life Coaching was relatively new then, and I didn't want to try it on my own, so my big sister, happy to have a few days away from her three little kids and husband, agreed to come with me for the introductory weekend. We hadn't had a chance to talk about any of the sessions all day, but when we got to dinner, we were just quiet. Then, I just asked her, "What did you think about the first session?"

My sister Sheryl, who is a pastor, is a little more conservative than I am, and I was worried about what she thought about these new ideas and concepts. But she also recognized the principles and was intrigued by the concepts. She also paused at the idea of being able to change whatever you didn't like about your life. She had all the same concerns I had. *What about prayer? What about God's will?* We talked about it all through dinner. When we got back to the room, we pulled out our Bibles and notebooks and started studying. We were searching for a principle to support this idea.

It took the entire weekend, but we came to the same conclusion. The principle was stewardship. A steward is given authority and responsibility to manage what they have been given. They manage in accordance with the guidelines the Master has laid out. The Master does not micromanage but is there to guide and support. I don't know why, but this was such an empowering thought. As long as I am following the principles, staying within my jurisdiction, and following Christ's example, I can decide what I want. I don't have to stay stuck in a bad situation. I could preside! This changed the way I thought about everything.

A steward is someone who believes they have been given the authority, by the Master, to move, trade, and make decisions. A steward does not act outside of the tenets of our faith. In fact, the opposite is true. A steward understands they have been *given permission and a mandate* to make their own decisions. They understand they can only exercise authority on matters within their jurisdiction. They know not to be bothered with matters that are outside of their jurisdiction. They know that when there are things that only God can do, they prayerfully wait for God to do it. When a steward is waiting on God, it is a conscious and intentional decision, and not just a default position because they feel that they have no other options.

There is one main characteristic that sets stewards apart from spectators: *fear*. Stewards do not operate from a place of fear. They are not afraid to take their authority and they are not afraid of taking responsibility for their actions and their decisions. They are not afraid to move about in the world and do what needs to be done, even if it is difficult or may cause disappointment or hurt feelings. Like spectators, stewards spend time in prayer with God, and they know His character. Stewards, however, inherently believe that God is good. They do not just say it and sing about it—they truly believe it. Stewards believe the Master to be fair, kind, and just, so they feel empowered to make decisions and are not fearful of making mistakes. When they do make mistakes, they don't fear the wrath of God or believe that they are out of the will of God. When they are unsure of what to do, stewards go back to the word of God to find out His original instruction or intent. At other times, they seek wise counsel from elders and mentors. Stewards believe they have been given everything they need to do what the Master has called them to do. As a result, they are intentional about being fruitful and multiplying what they have been given.

Being a steward does not mean that you operate perfectly. Like anything else, there are risks and disadvantages. When you have authority, it always comes with great responsibility. The steward is always at risk of making a mistake: some big and some small. As a judge, I know this reality all too well. There have been many times when I've made an incorrect ruling or made some other mistake. But I have not yet made a mistake that cannot be remedied by the higher courts. That's what they are there for—to put us back on track when we've made a mistake. That is what God does for us.

Think about the Prodigal Son. He made a terrible mistake and wound up so far off track he found himself in a pigpen. He could have wallowed there forever, but instead, he acknowledged his mistake. The Bible says when he was at his lowest point and contemplating eating what the pigs ate, "he came to his senses" (Luke 15:17 NIV). He thought about his father and his abundance. He then changed his mindset and became a steward. He took responsibility for his actions, got up, and ran back to his father. His father was not waiting to punish him, but ran out to meet him and had even planned a party celebrating the son's return. That's how God is. He sees our mistakes and is waiting for us to return to him. He lovingly guides us until we get back on track. The risk of making a mistake is a risk I am willing to take. The cost of living in fear is too high. I've wasted too much time praying about things that God has given me the authority to resolve. I have stayed too long in painful and unfulfilling situations to go back to waiting because I was too afraid to make a decision.

A steward welcomes responsibility. I mean, a steward is radical about responsibility. As a judge, I was responsible for everything that went on in the courtroom. I was responsible for making sure that all parties were treated fairly and that we got a just result. Many things happened that were out of my control. Nobody can control people, not even judges. People sometimes said and did things they weren't supposed to say or do. Sometimes there were delays and even mistrials. Sometimes life just happened—people were sick, there was a fire, or something else happened, but we still got things done in a timely manner. No matter what happened, I was responsible. I might not be at fault, but I was ultimately responsible. I looked for a remedy or a solution to what had gone wrong. I could have blamed someone or some circumstance, but it wouldn't have helped me get the process back on track and moving forward. A stewardship mindset requires radical responsibility over everything you have been given. When you know you're responsible for something, you take great care to manage it. Are you ready for radical responsibility?

RECESS

In what areas have you donned the mindset of a steward?
List the rewards of stewarding those areas.

Fear

Whether we admit it or not, we have all struggled with fear. Sometimes we are fearful about what we have been called to do or whether or not we are equipped to do it. Sometimes we are afraid of what people might think or say about us or just plain afraid that we will fail. My mentor told me that if you're not a little bit afraid about what's

Sidebar: "When I am afraid, I put my trust in you. In God, whose word I praise, in God I trust; I shall not be afraid. What can flesh do to me?" (Psalm 56:3-4 ESV)

next, you're not dreaming big enough. If you try enough things, you will certainly fail some of the time, but you won't die. I only became a judge because I tried and failed and tried again. There are so many scriptures about fear that it is clear that it is something we must steward. If we don't, we will never move from where we are.

RECESS

What have you always wanted to do, but have been afraid to do?
What is the worst-case scenario?
What is the best-case scenario?

The Spectator Mindset

A Spectator Mindset is believing that life is happening *to* us. Additionally, this mindset believes that we do not have the authority to change the things in our lives that we don't like. This mindset says that whatever is happening is God's will for us or is simply our cross to bear. This mindset encourages you to believe you are in the passenger seat of your life, observing what is happening. As a spectator, we do not believe we have permission, let alone the responsibility, to steer the car. We are all spectators in some area of our lives. This mindset is not always a simple matter of a person being frivolous or wanting to deny responsibility. Those with the spectator mindset don't take the wheel because they do not believe that they should. You've probably heard the saying *Jesus, take the wheel*. I know we often say it in jest, but often spectators really believe that Jesus is going to steer our lives. The problem with this is that Jesus is our example. We are to take the wheel and follow His example. When we are in this mindset, we are a victim of our circumstances. Sometimes we say that we are in a bad season. That is sometimes true. However, seasons change. When a season of lack persists for years and even decades, it has become a state of being. Persistent lack is not what God wants for us. God created us to be fruitful and to multiply. The only way we can do that is to take our authority and accept our responsibility to steward that area of lack.

I cannot count the times a defendant has stood before me and said, "It wasn't my fault. It is because of him, them, or it, that I did what I did." Or, "This person made me do it." I have counseled and coached many people who have wanted to change something in their lives but didn't believe they had the power to do so. Instead, they blamed spouses, children, employers, and friends for why they could not take responsibility to make change happen.

Have you ever said that someone made you mad, or made you tell them off, or act out in some way? I certainly have. I know you've heard someone say that how they behave or what they do or don't have is because of their parents, or where they were raised, or because all men or all women are bad, or some other variant of blame. At the end of the day, they are blaming someone or something outside of themselves. They are waiting on some external force to change their lives when, really, only they can take responsibility to change their lives from the inside out. Where there is no responsibility, there can be no authority.

It might be easy to look at those caught up in the criminal justice system and think, *Well, yes. They need to take responsibility for their actions.*

But I have experienced this same mindset with believers as well. For example, many believers have the mindset that every circumstance they encounter is God's will. Never mind that they made a mistake in judgment, or just made a poor decision, like getting into an unhealthy relationship, or making a poor investment or ill-fated business venture. I'm sure we all have heard a person testify about getting a house or car that they knew they couldn't afford and how this was a blessing from God. That was great until a few months into it when they realized it was a mistake.

Instead of acknowledging the mistake, this discussion quickly turns to either it being the Devil's fault or God's divine plan. It is so true that God can bring us through hard times, but many of the hard times we blame on God or the Devil are our own doing. My point is that the person with a spectator mindset is not inclined to take responsibility for their actions and, therefore, cannot take authority to remedy the situation. Not because they don't want to, but because they don't believe they have a right to do so. They are waiting for Jesus to take the wheel.

This mindset is so disempowering. When you cannot take responsibility, you cannot change course or remedy the mistake. With this mindset, we feel that we have no choice but to wait on God because we believe it is God or the Devil who put us there. The spectator may have you believe that you have to wait for God to rescue you, or send you a sign so that you can move on from your mistake. As spectators, we can spend months, years, and even decades praying and waiting for God to rescue us from situations that God has empowered us to remedy on our own. Remember, it's like driving a car into a ditch and then just waiting and praying for God to rescue us when we could simply put the car in reverse, back up, and go in a different direction. Sure, there may be damage to the car. We may need to re-evaluate how we got off course, but we don't have to stay stuck in the ditch.

Let me illustrate how this may look in real life:

- "God, you knew I wanted to be in a good marriage. I trusted you. How could you let me end up with this awful man/woman?"
- "The Devil didn't want me in this career, so he kept me from finishing college."
- "The Devil sent this circumstance to destroy my dreams."
- "I am no longer growing in this ministry. I really want to go, but I'll wait ten years for a sign from God."
- "If God didn't want me to do this, He would have closed this door."
- "I know I'm mean, but this is just how I am. My momma was like this. Her mama was like this. This is just how we are."

These are all actual statements from real people blaming someone or something for how their life is unfolding. And instead of stewarding that area, they are waiting for something, anything, to happen.

You cannot take responsibility while casting blame. Being a Steward requires radical responsibility.

I recently heard a prominent Christian leader, after being caught in a compromising position, proclaim, "God had to bring me to this place so that I can grow." God can certainly use everything we go through and make it work for our good. But blaming God for our poor decisions will keep us stuck in the ditch and repeating these poor decisions.

Sidebar: You cannot take responsibility while casting blame. Being a Steward requires radical responsibility.

Many spectators remain in relationships, states of mind, and at churches or in jobs that no longer meet their needs, facilitate growth, or at times are even abusive. It's not that we enjoy these situations, but it's because we feel powerless to change them. The Spectator Mindset dictates that they must wait until something, someone, or God changes things for them.

This mindset is rooted in fear. Many people find it difficult to make tough decisions, out of fear of disappointing or hurting people's feelings. Many believers are afraid to make decisions because they believe they will disappoint or anger God. This rationale belies the basic premise of our faith that God is good. A good God is not waiting to rain down wrath because of a simple mistake. That is why certain beliefs are necessary as we take the journey from spectator to steward. Maybe we have to take a closer look at what it is we really believe about God.

We will never be perfect. Even if we pray and fast, we will sometimes make mistakes, bad choices, or even stupid choices. I have before, and I'm sure I will again. We are all human. Instead of taking responsibility for those choices, a lot of people turn it into providence, saying, "It had to be this way," or, "It is God's will." We know God can forgive our mistakes and redeem and restore us. The only way to learn and grow from our mistakes is to take responsibility for them. If we do not, we are destined to repeat them.

The result of being a spectator is being stuck and suffering lack. Remember when the servant placed the talent in the ground? When we are stuck, we are not progressing, nor are we fruitful. We are suffering from lack. If you've been praying and waiting for something for years or decades, you may want to consider whether you have become a spectator in this area. Instead of taking responsibility to decide whether to change course, or remedy a situation, you may have abdicated your responsibility to God, the circumstance, or the Devil.

This is not really surprising, given the fact that many of the songs we sing and the messages we've heard over the years in church suggest God will solve all of our problems. We are warned not to get ahead of God's timing for fear of His wrath. We're encouraged not to take action because "God's gonna make a way out of no way". God will open doors and turn crooked paths straight.

Listen, I believe God can do all of these things. In fact, I've experienced it. I have been encouraged by these songs and messages and I have preached some of these messages myself. I just want to make sure that when God does His part, by opening a door and making a crooked path straight, we are ready to do our part and walk through that open door and drive on that straight path. We were created to be fruitful and multiply. We can't do that if we're sitting around waiting. God can never fail to do His part. Are you doing your part?

RECESS

Is there an area in your life where you have not been fruitful?
Have you felt like a spectator in this area?
How can you begin to steward this area?

CHAPTER 10

Jurisdiction and Boundaries

What Is Jurisdiction?

Jurisdiction is the most powerful concept to keep in mind when presiding. As you are becoming a steward, you must learn when and where to exercise your authority. Merely putting on the robe does not make you a judge. There is a lot to learn. Jurisdiction is the area over which you have the authority to rule, govern, or make decisions. Jurisdiction sets clear boundaries. It defines what a judge can and must do. But maybe even more importantly, it makes clear what a judge *cannot* do. A steward is most confident when they know exactly what they can and cannot do. If you don't address the question of jurisdiction first, you are likely to set yourself up for failure. When everyone knows what they can and cannot do, there is order. For me, there is nothing worse than feeling powerless or simply not knowing what to do. Have you ever been in a situation personally or professionally when you had no idea what to do? How did you feel? I hate feeling this way. Do I attempt to do something, or do I wait? Some who feel this way will do nothing. Some will do just about anything. They will do anything they have seen someone else doing. They take advice from anyone and everyone and usually end up making a bigger mess that may take even longer to resolve than the original situation. Knowing your jurisdiction will provide clarity so that you always know what to do and what *not* to do. Knowing your jurisdiction changes the way you think, what you say, how you feel, and what you do or don't do. Most importantly, knowing your jurisdiction changes the way you pray!

Jurisdiction establishes order. Our government, organizations, businesses, and even churches cannot be effective without order. In a courtroom, there will be order. Have you ever wondered how the most complex and emotional cases can be discussed and resolved in court? The nastiest divorce, the most complex contract dispute, or even the most heinous of crimes, can be discussed and resolved in court because there is order.

There are times when judges receive cases that we may not want to deal with. It may be the subject matter, the procedural posture, or even the lawyers that rub you the wrong way. In one particular case, it was all three. I was dealing with a case that was procedurally very complicated. It was a relatively new area of law, so there was not a lot of guidance. I didn't necessarily dislike either of the lawyers, but they didn't get along, and whenever they were paired on a case, it was contentious. Even something as simple as a request for a continuance by either party was always met with a strenuous objection and argument.

So, when my clerk reminded me that the matter was on this particular morning, I was not happy. I always had this pair meet me in chambers before going on the record, so I could try to iron out any issues before we started.

The phone rang. "I sent the lawyers back."

"I know. I can hear them arguing already."

When they got to the door, I invited them to have a seat. I took a deep breath. "Okay folks, where are we on this case?"

Both started talking at once. I was just not in the mood to have this rancor start my day. After twenty minutes, we had gotten nowhere. Both sides were still entrenched over what was the proper procedure for going forward. I told the lawyers I would continue the case and each lawyer could submit a written brief, and I would make a decision.

In the meantime, I did some research and consulted some colleagues. Unfortunately, they gave me differing opinions about how to handle the matter. I fretted over this case for two full weeks, trying to decide what to do. I decided to go back to the beginning and look at all the first filings of the case. I came across a document that everyone, including me, had missed. This document changed everything. The bottom line was that I didn't have jurisdiction over this matter at this time. Therefore, no decision I could make would have any impact on this matter until a higher court made a decision. It solved all of my problems, and it would have been funny if I hadn't wasted so much time fretting over an issue over which I had no jurisdiction.

Understanding jurisdiction will save you valuable time, energy, and even aggravation. When we say that a circumstance is our cross to bear or just a season we are going through, we often skip asking the question of jurisdiction. If we don't ask that question, we can waste precious time waiting for a change of season or for a burden to be lifted. If God has jurisdiction, meaning that only He can address the situation, then we simply must steward the wait. If you have jurisdiction, you have a duty to steward. You can pray and get God's plan or strategy to navigate your way through the situation, but if you have jurisdiction, no amount of waiting will change that. No need to waste months, years, and even decades in a season that was never really your season, or carrying a burden that was never yours to carry, just because you failed to determine whether or not you had jurisdiction.

When you understand the importance of jurisdiction, you will no longer waste time worrying about things you cannot change. Instead, you will spend more time doing only those things you are supposed to do. Most of the time, when I am coaching or ministering to people, they express how they feel helpless or frustrated because they are in the middle of a situation or circumstance in which they feel they have no control. My first question is always about jurisdiction. We can't do anything until we establish jurisdiction.

I recently had a case where I wanted to grant the request of one of the litigants. The request was reasonable and seemed fair in my judgment. However, a higher court had ruled that a previous order must stand. As much as I wanted to change this order, it was simply out of my jurisdiction.

Do I have jurisdiction over this issue I am trying to address or change? That's what every judge asks before hearing any case. The reason this question is so important is that we only have so much time and energy for each day and our lifetime. It is important to spend that time and energy on things where we *can* have an impact: things that we really want and can accomplish. This reminds me of the opening lines of what is often referred to as the Serenity Prayer, frequently attributed to Reinhold Niebuhr:

God, grant me the serenity to accept the things I cannot change,
courage to change the things I can,
and wisdom to know the difference.

The serenity prayer is a well-known prayer often quoted by those in recovery. I have found this prayer is also helpful when we look at the principle of stewardship. This prayer of serenity demonstrates that there are some things you can change and some things that you cannot change. It is a reminder that it takes courage to do what you are supposed to do and you must be at peace with the things you cannot change. Most importantly, you need the wisdom to know the difference. Knowing your jurisdiction is the difference.

Most of the things we spend time on are really things that we cannot change. *Why doesn't this person like me? How will this person respond? Why didn't I take that opportunity?* Have you ever spent days, weeks, months, or years worrying about something that you cannot change? Knowing where to spend your time and energy and knowing when something is out of your jurisdiction is a game-changer.

There are three things you need to know when it comes to understanding and exercising your jurisdiction:

- The biblical origin of jurisdiction.
- What is in God's jurisdiction?
- What is in your jurisdiction?

Once you understand this, you will never be unsure of what to do again. You will know when to steward and when to wait on the Lord. I promise that this will save you countless weeks, months, and even decades of worrying and waiting. You can spend that same time and energy on doing, becoming, and having everything that God planned for you before the foundation of the earth.

RECESS

Is there an area in your life where you can pray for serenity to accept something that you have no jurisdiction to steward?
Is there an area in your life where you can pray for courage to steward what is in your jurisdiction?
Is there an area where you can pray for wisdom to know the difference?

Origins of Jurisdiction

In the book of Genesis, God lays out the origins of our jurisdiction. He tells us what He is responsible for and what we, as humankind, will be responsible for. Every steward receives authority from a higher power. As a judge, I received my authority to preside over a department from the State of California. As a follower of Christ, my authority to preside over my own life comes from Genesis 1.

The creation story is a blueprint for creating order. In Genesis 1 (NLT), God established jurisdiction when he created the universe. In addition to establishing boundaries, God's jurisdiction created roles and responsibilities and established the principles by which every area of the universe would be governed. Establishing boundaries, authority, roles, and responsibilities is a construct that every successful society, institution, and organization has duplicated since then. Whether you've been walking with Christ for a while or are new to the family of God, I encourage you to hang in there with me as we review a few scriptures. Remember, the word of God is a living word and, no matter how many times you read it, God can reveal something new.

"In the beginning God created the heavens and the earth. The earth was formless and empty, and darkness covered the deep waters. And the Spirit of God was hovering over the surface of the waters" (Genesis 1: 1-2, NLT).

In the beginning, there was only God, and He is, therefore, the authority over all He created—heaven, earth, the galaxies, the cosmos, and every creature therein. That includes you and me. However, before God created humanity or any other creature, he established jurisdiction. God observed that the earth was formless, empty, and dark.

"Then God said, 'Let there be light,' and there was light. And God saw that the light was good. Then he separated the light from the darkness. God called the light 'day' and the darkness 'night.' And evening passed and morning came, marking the first day" (Genesis 1: 3-5, NLT)

God then began establishing jurisdiction by assigning roles and responsibilities, and by naming and setting boundaries for His creation. The light would be called *day* and the darkness *night* and each would do only what it was supposed to do.

"Then God said, 'Let there be a space between the waters, to separate the waters of the heavens from the waters of the earth.' And that is what happened. God made this space to separate the waters of the earth from the waters of the heavens. God called the space 'sky'" (Genesis 1: 6-8, NLT).

When God separated the waters and created a vault in the sky, each knew their role, responsibility, and jurisdiction. God continued to name, set boundaries, and give responsibility to His creation in verses 9 and 10.

"Then God said, 'Let the waters beneath the sky flow together into one place, so dry ground may appear.' And that is what happened. God called the dry ground 'land' and the waters 'seas.' And God saw that it was good" (Genesis 1: 9-10, NLT).

After the structure was in place and the sky, the land, and the seas knew their roles, God gave them the responsibility to do only what they were created to do. In verses 11–12, God gave the plants and trees the responsibility to reproduce after their own kind. When they did, God saw that it was good.

"Then God said, 'Let the land sprout with vegetation—every sort of seed-bearing plant, and trees that grow seed-bearing fruit. These seeds will then produce the kinds of plants and trees from which they came.' And that is what happened. The land produced vegetation—all sorts of seed-bearing plants, and trees with seed-bearing fruit. Their seeds produced plants and trees of the same kind. And God saw that it was good" (Genesis 1: 11-12, NLT).

On the third day, God told the lights to appear in the sky to separate the day from night, giving each its own jurisdiction.

"And evening passed and morning came, marking the third day. Then God said, 'Let lights appear in the sky to separate the day from the night. Let them be signs to mark the seasons, days, and years. Let these lights in the sky shine down on the earth.' And that is what happened. God made two great lights—the larger one to govern the day, and the smaller one to govern the night. He also made the stars. God set these lights in the sky to light the earth, to govern the day and night, and to separate the light from the darkness. And God saw that it was good."

"And evening passed and morning came, marking the fourth day" (Genesis 1: 13-19, NLT).

After seeing what He had done was good, God created creatures to occupy the earth and gave each creature a role, responsibilities, and jurisdiction. Each did only what they were supposed to do.

"Then God said, 'Let the waters swarm with fish and other life. Let the skies be filled with birds of every kind.' So God created great sea creatures and every living thing that scurries and swarms in the water, and every sort of bird—each producing offspring of the same kind. And God saw that it was good. Then God blessed them, saying, 'Be fruitful and multiply. Let the fish fill the seas, and let the birds multiply on the earth.'"

"And evening passed and morning came, marking the fifth day."

"Then God said, 'Let the earth produce every sort of animal, each producing offspring of the same kind—livestock, small animals that scurry along the ground, and wild animals.' And that is what happened. God made all sorts of wild animals, livestock, and small animals, each able to produce offspring of the same kind. And God saw that it was good" (Genesis 1: 20-25, NLT).

Finally, in verse 26, after the stage had been set, God created man/woman. The process did not change. He gave us roles, responsibilities, and jurisdiction.

"Then God said, 'Let us make human beings in our image, to be like us. They will reign over the fish in the sea, the birds in the sky, the livestock, all the wild animals on the earth, and the small animals that scurry along the ground.'"

"So God created human beings in his own image. In the image of God he created them; male and female he created them. Then God blessed them and said, 'Be fruitful and multiply. Fill the earth and govern it. Reign over the fish in the sea, the birds in the sky, and all the animals that scurry along the ground.'"

"Then God said, 'Look! I have given you every seed-bearing plant throughout the earth and all the fruit trees for your food. And I have given every green plant as food for all the wild animals, the birds in the sky, and the small animals that scurry along the ground—everything that has life.' And that is what happened."

"Then God looked over all he had made, and he saw that it was very good! And evening passed and morning came, marking the sixth day" (Genesis 1: 26-31, NLT).

The principle that God established during the creation story is simple. Presiding over the universe, God observed what was out of order. He spoke, declared His authority, and created everything. Everything He created, he gave a role, responsibilities, and jurisdiction, thus creating order. Fish did not take flight and birds did not venture to the bottom of the seas. The sun did not shine by night, nor the moon by day. Everything functioned as he established it.

When God finally creates human beings in verse 27, jurisdiction had been established and man was given two responsibilities:

- To be fruitful and increase;
- To subdue the earth and rule over or preside over it and everything that occupies the earth.

I submit to you that when God breathed life into us. He gave us jurisdiction over every part of our being: our bodies, our souls, and our spirits. In other words, God created us to be stewards of what He has given to us. His plan did not include coming to earth and micromanaging us or making our decisions for us. When we preside, we take stewardship over everything we are given authority over, and the result is that we should be fruitful. The creation story is a precedent, not only in organizations and institutions like the courtroom but also for us individually. God ordained the principle of stewardship in the beginning. Are you ready to be the steward God created you to be?

What Is in God's Jurisdiction?

Now that we understand the origins of our authority to steward, let's look at what is in God's jurisdiction. One could argue that since God is sovereign, *everything* is in His jurisdiction. I would agree with that. However, remember that God gave us free will and chose to rule by:

- providing instructions and teachings in His word,
- sending an example in Christ Jesus,
- and sending His Holy Spirit to empower us.

Therefore, God retained jurisdiction over some things and delegated to us jurisdiction over other things. For example, whatever seems impossible for us is usually something in God's jurisdiction. It is good to know that what we cannot do, God is well able to do. The best thing about understanding God's jurisdiction is knowing that

He will never fail to do His part (Isaiah 26:2-4, Psalm 73:26, and Revelation 1:18). It is also important to know that whenever we are trying to do something that is in God's jurisdiction, we are out of order.

Time

The first thing that God retained jurisdiction over is time. When we spend time worrying about something that has already happened, or what might happen in the future, we are not only out of order, but we are wasting time and energy we could be using to address what *is* in our jurisdiction. The only thing in our jurisdiction is the present—how we choose to respond to what is happening right now.

The Past

"Do not remember the former things, Nor consider the things of old. Behold, I will do a new thing, Now it shall spring forth; Shall you not know it? I will even make a road in the wilderness *And* rivers in the desert," (Isaiah 43:18-19 NKJV).

You may be spending a lot of time reliving and relitigating past mistakes. *Why did I leave? Why did I stay? Why did I say that? Why didn't I stop?* This is called *regret*. It is a profound sadness or disappointment over something that you cannot change. It can lead to depression, despondency, and an overall feeling of helplessness. I have certainly looked back on things I wish I'd done or said differently. But we have no jurisdiction and therefore no power over the past. Time spent wishing things could be different is a waste of our time and energy. Instead of dwelling on my mistakes and allowing them to be a prison that keeps me from going forward, I look at them as a school, where I can learn what to do or not do next time. This way, you never lose, you only learn.

So even if some circumstance in the past looked like a failure or a setback at the time, God can use it now to propel you forward.

RECESS

Have you ever made a mistake or miscalculation that has made you fearful to try that thing again?
What lessons can you learn from that situation that can help you do things differently in the future?
(The following scriptures may be helpful: Isaiah 46:10, 2 Peter 3:8, Ephesians 1:4, Philippians 4:6-7, 1 Peter 5:7)

The Future

"Therefore, do not worry about tomorrow, for tomorrow will worry about itself. Each day has enough trouble of its own," (Matthew 6:34 NIV).

The future is also in God's jurisdiction. While we can and should plan and prepare for our future, we cannot control anything in the future. We are out of order when we become anxious about something that may or may not happen. I have done my share of fretting about what could or should happen. Ninety-five percent or more of what I have fretted about never came to be. And even if it did, it wasn't nearly as bad as I imagined it to be. When I find myself worrying about what may or may not happen, this is what I do—instead of imagining the worst that can happen, I use that time to imagine the best-case scenario of what could happen. When you consistently imagine the worst-case scenario, you will probably experience it. After calamity befell Job, he said, "What I always feared has happened to me. What I dreaded has come true" (Job 3:25 NLT). If you're going to take time to think about the future, think about what you want, not what you don't want.

RECESS

What do you find yourself worrying about?
Take three to five minutes and imagine the best-case scenario.
How you would like that situation to be?

People

People are solely in God's jurisdiction. We cannot control people any more than we can control the weather. As much as we might want to, we can't control what people think or how they feel about us. And we definitely can't control what they say about us. These things are none of our business and are outside of our jurisdiction.

As a judge, I had no jurisdiction over what people thought or how they felt. I could order them to obey my rulings, but I couldn't order how they should think or feel about me or my rulings. What's cool is that I didn't have to. I could only regulate how people conducted themselves in my courtroom. I could determine how they addressed me and how they treated my staff. If they were disrespectful or could not follow the rules of the court, I could have them removed from my presence, fined, and/or put in custody for being in contempt of court.

I wish I had this same authority outside of the courtroom! Believe me, if I could put people in jail for talking loudly on their cell phones while in a movie or a restaurant, I would. But I have no jurisdiction over people outside of my courtroom. However, it is within your jurisdiction to decide how you will be treated. I recognize you cannot send someone to jail, but you can set a standard for how you will allow yourself to be treated. If people choose to be disrespectful, consistently ignore healthy boundaries, or disregard your feelings, then they may have to be removed from your presence until they can demonstrate that they will treat you the way you deserve to be treated. If I encounter someone who consistently ignores my boundaries, I choose distance over disrespect. That is, I limit or eliminate the time and energy I spend with that person. When someone is not treating you like you deserve to be treated, you don't have to cuss or fuss. Creating distance will speak volumes and give you peace.

RECESS

Do you allow others to dictate your mood and what you do?
How can you begin to steward your responses to others?
Have you set boundaries for how you want to be treated?
Do you allow people to cross those boundaries?
If so, how can you choose distance over disrespect?

To help with this exercise, download a copy of the Know Your Jurisdiction Worksheet by going to:
shelynabrown.com/preside-thebookworksheets

Circumstances

Even if we are good stewards, there are still things we cannot control. When the pandemic hit, everyone was thrown into chaos. I knew many who wasted a lot of time and energy by fighting the circumstances and only ended up frustrated and angry. Many recognized that this circumstance was out of their jurisdiction and decided to preside over what they could. Some presided over their response to the pandemic and used this time to get healthy and take some much-needed rest, and some picked up a new skill like learning to cook. During this time, I thought about the serenity prayer. This was a circumstance that I could not change. Being upset about it was a waste of time. I decided that while I could not change what was happening, I could preside over my time while I was home. I got serious about writing this book. After all, I couldn't leave my home for several weeks. Knowing your jurisdiction saves your limited time and energy to use on the things that will help you to be fruitful.

RECESS

Which circumstances that are out of your jurisdiction are you trying to control?

How can you preside over your response to those circumstances?

CHAPTER 11

What Is in Our Jurisdiction?

"May God himself, the God of peace, sanctify you through and through. May your whole spirit, soul and body be kept blameless at the coming of our Lord Jesus Christ" (I Thessalonians 5:23 NIV).

You may be wondering, *What is in my jurisdiction?* I was searching for a deep and meaningful answer, but the answer is very simple. When God breathed life into us, He gave us jurisdiction over all that we are. We are tripartite beings. We are spirits; we have a soul, and we are housed in a body. With our spirit, the eternal part of us, we can relate to and commune with God. With our soul—the mind, will, and emotions—we can relate to ourselves. With our body, we see, hear, taste, touch, and smell to relate to the world around us. Each part of us is intricately woven together. God's will for every part of us is to flourish and prosper. God left us instructions over each of these areas to steward and reap abundance. I would submit to you that whenever God left an instruction, He meant us to follow it. Therefore, if there is an instruction, you have the jurisdiction, the authority, and a duty to exercise it. That is your jurisdiction.

Body

"Don't you realize that your body is the temple of the Holy Spirit, who lives in you and was given to you by God? You do not belong to yourself, for God bought you with a high price. So you must honor God with your body" (I Corinthians 6:19-20 NLT).

The first thing God gave us stewardship over was the body. He formed us in His own image. He breathed the breath of life into us and then He gave us stewardship over it. We are to treat our body like a temple and use it in the way He intended—to glorify Him. This seems like an obvious one, but you would be surprised at how many people don't realize they are responsible for stewarding their own bodies.

My mother has had several knee surgeries on the same knee. My sister and I, as we've gotten older, each began to experience pain in the same knee. My first thought was, *Well, it's just hereditary. There's nothing I can do.* Whenever I felt a little pain, I would start thinking about preparing for knee surgery. I stopped doing certain exercises out of fear and my knee kept getting worse. Then I remembered that I have the authority to steward this area, just like any other. I began to be a better steward by doing exercises to strengthen my knee. And now, I only speak of health and well-being about that part of my body. Instead of giving up, I'm doing my part as a steward. What about you? Is there a part of your body or an area in your health that you have not managed or have given up on managing because you think there is no hope? Have you become a spectator?

Diabetes, joint pain, migraines, and mental health concerns are all things we often neglect because we believe that if mamma or daddy had it, then we have to have it too. If you just give up and remain a spectator in that area, I guarantee there will be lack and you are likely to experience what you have always observed. Let me invite you to be a steward of that area and see what happens.

RECESS

In what ways have you been a good steward of your temple?
In what ways can you steward the areas you have
previously been a spectator?
What is a small thing you can do to better steward your temple?

Spirit

"For those who live according to the flesh set their minds on the things of the flesh, but those who live according to the Spirit set their minds on the things of the Spirit. For to set the mind on the flesh is death, but to set the mind on the Spirit is life and peace. For the mind that is set on the flesh is hostile to God, for it does not submit to God's law; indeed, it cannot. Those who are in the flesh cannot please God" (Romans 8:5-8 ESV).

God is Spirit. The only way that we can relate to God and receive from him is through our spirit. "God is spirit, and those who worship him must worship in spirit and truth" (John 4:24 ESV). Because our spirit is intangible, we often don't think about how to manage it. We think that it is something God will take care of. But our spirit is something that God entrusted to us. In Romans 8:5, scripture makes it clear that we can choose to live according to the flesh or according to the spirit. It reminds us that to set our mind to the flesh is death, but the mind set on the spirit is life and peace. The spirit is in our jurisdiction and we must preside over it. God cannot give us a harvest unless we plant a good seed in the ground and nurture it. We will know when we have been a good steward of our spirit because we will see evidence of that fruit in our lives. Galatians 5:22-23 (ESV) says, "But the fruit of the Spirit is love, joy, peace, patience, kindness, goodness, faithfulness, gentleness, self-control; against such things there is no law."

In a church that I attended while at college, there was a standing joke about one of the church mothers who was always praying. She prayed throughout the church service. She prayed in her car and even at the grocery store. The joke was that she was always so mean! No one ever wanted to talk to her or ask her anything. How could anyone who prayed *that* much be so mean? Praying and fasting are good spiritual disciplines, but they do not necessarily make us spiritual. The fruit of the spirit is the measure of how spiritual we are. Therefore, we must also steward the fruit of the spirit. Are you experiencing love, joy, and peace? Are you exercising patience, kindness, goodness, and faithfulness? It is when we can see evidence of the fruit of the spirit that we know we have been good stewards of our spirit.

For more guidance about each fruit of the Spirit, take a look at the following verses:

- Love: John 3:15
- Joy: Psalm 16:11
- Peace: Isaiah 26:3, 2 Thessalonians 3:16
- Patience: Romans 8:25, Galatians 6:9
- Kindness: Ephesians 4:32, Proverbs 11:17
- Goodness: Psalm 23:6, Psalm 27:13
- Faithfulness: Proverbs 28:20, Luke 16:10-12, 2 Corinthians 5:7
- Gentleness: Proverbs 15:1, Titus 3:2
- Self-control: Proverbs 25:28, 2 Timothy 1:7, Proverbs 16:32

Recess

In what ways have you been a good steward of your spirit?
List the evidence.
How can you be a better steward and experience more
love, joy, and peace?
Where can you be a better steward and exercise more patience,
kindness, goodness, and faithfulness?

Soul

Thoughts

"Casting down arguments and every high thing that exalts itself against the knowledge of God, bringing every thought into captivity to the obedience of Christ" (2 Corinthians 10:5 NKJV).

The soul is made up of our mind, our will, and our emotions. Our thoughts, beliefs, desires, and perceptions flow from the mind. In managing our soul, I can't think of an area more important to manage than our thoughts. Our thoughts create our reality. They have more power than we think. Think about the last thing that really made you laugh out loud. Just take a minute, close your eyes, and remember the joke or the image. How did you feel when you remembered it? Did you begin to smile? Did you chuckle or even laugh out loud? It works the same way when you think of sad, worrying, or anxious thoughts. Our thoughts are so powerful they influence our emotions. Our thoughts plus our emotions dictate what we do or don't do. I like to think of it as an equation that I call TEA:

Thoughts + Emotions = Actions/Inaction

Think of a project that you need to get done—something that you've done successfully before and you feel confident that you can complete successfully again. That *thought* stimulates *feelings* of confidence. When you feel more confident, you are more likely to take positive *action*. If there is a project that you *think* will be difficult, maybe something you have struggled with in the past and you feel that you may not be competent to complete it, you are more likely to *procrastinate* or find excuses not to do the task. Our thoughts are powerful. For example, whenever I'm asked to teach or do some training in an area of my expertise, I can usually prepare for it quickly and painlessly. I enjoy teaching and training, and I've received great feedback about my presentations. My *thoughts* immediately go to all of my successes in that area and I *feel* confident and inspired to get things *done*. If I'm asked to prepare or present a project that involves numbers or percentages, I immediately *think* about how I struggled with math in college. I *feel* incompetent and not qualified, so I *procrastinate*. Does this sound familiar? What we think influences how we feel, which determines how and whether or not we will act.

There are numerous verses to support how powerful our thoughts are. According to scripture, our thoughts can create our reality. They determine whether or not we will have peace, "You keep him in perfect peace whose mind is stayed on you, because he trusts in you" (Isaiah 26:3 ESV), or whether we will be stable enough to navigate our world, "He is a double-minded man, unstable in all his ways," (James 1:8 ESV). Ultimately, our thoughts determine the quality of our life and who we will become, "For as he thinks in his heart, so *is* he" (Proverbs 23:7 NKJV).

We become what we consistently think about. This should make us want to preside over our thoughts and consider what we're thinking about. If you like who you are and the quality of your life, stay with that train of thought. If there is anything that you are dissatisfied with, the good news is that you can change it!

In 2 Corinthians 10:5 (ESV), Paul talks to the people at Corinth. "We destroy arguments and every lofty opinion raised against the knowledge of God, and take every thought captive to obey Christ." He explains his apostolic authority allows him to bring every thought into captivity and make it obey Christ. We have the same authority and duty to do the same. I have heard this scripture many times, but no one has ever explained to me how to do it. I'm going to share with you how I do it.

One day, when I was presiding over a very complex murder trial, it occurred to me that Paul exercises his authority over thoughts in the same way I exercise my judicial authority over every piece of evidence that is presented in a trial. A trial is the most important right in our justice system. A person charged with a crime has a right to go through this formal procedure, where nothing is taken for granted and every piece of evidence will be examined. In a trial, everybody is sworn to do their part. The prosecutor is tasked with proving every element of the case beyond a reasonable doubt. The defense attorney's job is to defend her client against all the charges. The jury's job is to determine the facts and decide guilt or innocence based on those facts. I may be biased, but I think the most important role is that of the judge. That is because she decides *which* facts the jury will hear.

Paul says that we should destroy arguments and opinions that are contrary to the knowledge of God. In essence, if the thought is not in alignment with what God says, it is stricken. As a judge, that is exactly what I do. Any piece of evidence, any statement, observation, or piece of demonstrative evidence that is not in alignment with the laws of California is stricken (removed) from the official records. For example, some evidence, like hearsay, is simply not reliable enough to be presented in a trial. An example of hearsay would be that you heard that people in your family or neighborhood aren't cut out to do certain things or hold certain jobs. Hearsay is like the old game of Telephone (also known as Chinese Whispers). Someone says something and they pass it on to the next person. By the time the statement gets to the last person, it is distorted in some way. Hearsay is unreliable and a good judge will strike it from the record. Sometimes, certain things and even statistics are just not relevant and can be excluded. My counselor may have been right about the fact that folks from my neighborhood usually don't excel or go into certain fields. However, her facts were completely irrelevant to me fulfilling my purpose. If God has called you to do something, facts and statistics are not relevant. Don't allow irrelevant and unreliable information to create arguments in your head. If you are thinking that you are inadequate or not capable, those are opinions that are in direct conflict with what God says about you and you should strike those thoughts.

It is a lot of work to preside over a trial. You are not passively listening, you are focussing all of your attention and energy, listening to every word, and making tough decisions in real time. You are taking errant arguments captive. But it is necessary if you want the right verdict at the end of a trial. If you allow in erroneous or incompetent evidence, then there will be an unjust verdict. Don't let a thoughtless comment from someone when you were eight years old, or a statistic about your age, race, or gender, make you believe you cannot be, do, or have something that God says you can be, do, or have. There is nothing more important than presiding over your thoughts and only allowing in thoughts that are in alignment with what God says about you.

Our minds are amazing. Studies by researchers at Queens University, Canada suggest that we have 6,200 thoughts per day (Craig, 2020). That is a lot to preside over. What makes it even more difficult is that not every thought you think is true. Really think about that. Just because you have a thought doesn't mean it's true. My grandmother used to say, "You can't keep a bird from flying over your head, but you can make sure it doesn't make a nest in your hair." That means that you may not be able to control what thoughts pop into your head, but you can control which ones you allow to linger.

You are not your thoughts. You can decide the thoughts on which you want to ruminate. Selecting only competent and reliable thoughts is key. One place to start is the word of God. Does the thought you're thinking about a subject line up with what God says about it? Are you really inadequate, or are you fearfully and wonderfully made? Are you really incompetent and unable to do something, or can you do all things through Christ who strengthens you? It really just comes down to being selective about what you think. If you're interested in or would like a more in-depth discussion about the science of the mind and how our thoughts affect us, please read, *Switch On Your Brain: The Key to Peak Happiness, Thinking, and Health* (Leaf, 2015). Dr. Caroline Leaf is a neuroscientist who reveals how Scripture can help us renew our minds.

Here is an exercise that I use to help me manage my thoughts. Imagine being at a buffet. Would you put food on your plate that you don't like or know will cause an allergic reaction? No. Then why would you pile on your plate thoughts that make you feel resentful, jealous, sad, or fearful? I'm allergic to tomatoes, but please, pile more on my plate! It's not that disempowering thoughts don't come. You can see the tomatoes in the tray, but you don't have to pile them onto your plate! Why meditate on the thoughts you know will make you sick?

RECESS

Thoughts + Emotions = Action/Inaction
Are you surprised you could steward your thoughts?
How have you been a good steward of your thoughts?
What was the result?
Have you ever been a spectator and allowed your thoughts
to take you to a place you didn't want to go?
In what ways can you be a better steward of your thoughts?

Emotions

What about our emotions? You're probably thinking, *She's not suggesting I can steward my emotions, is she? I can't help it when I'm sad or depressed. It's not my fault if someone makes me mad.*

These are things I used to believe until I saw the Bible's instructions about emotions. What do instructions in the Bible mean? That we have the authority and duty to preside over that area by following the instruction. The Bible instructs us on how to address our emotions. (See Appendix B for further details.) Jesus demonstrated emotions by showing empathy and compassion for those He encountered and healed. He felt sadness and wept at the tomb of Lazarus. Jesus demonstrated anger when he turned over tables in the temple. "You serpents, you brood of vipers, how are you to escape being sentenced to hell?" (Matthew 23:33 ESV).

Emotions are not good or bad. They do not have the intellect, or care about facts, or what is true or relevant. Since our thoughts influence our emotions, emotions are really just a gauge of what you've been thinking about. If you want to know what you've been thinking about, notice how you're feeling. Whether you are overwhelmed, sad and depressed, or joyful and peaceful, it is because of what you have been thinking. Ignoring emotions is like ignoring your gas gauge. The gauge is only an indicator of where you are. Ignoring that it is on empty won't change the fact that you are about to run out of gas. Not too long ago, I was in a situation where I ignored my gauge and did not preside over my emotions. I was being a spectator. I allowed my emotions to manage me and it was not a good experience. I was annoyed when a colleague questioned how I handled something in a meeting I was hosting. They emailed a 'helpful' suggestion. I responded, explaining that what I did was by design and the reason for doing it the way I did. I was irritated because I didn't feel like I should have had to explain myself. It was my meeting. Instead of just quashing the issue, my colleague went on to tell me how their way of handling it would have been better. I didn't appreciate the advice or the tone. I offered to discuss it over the phone because, clearly, they did not understand what I was saying. The emails went back and forth until I finally snapped and said I thought they were being quite offensive.

I should have let it go, but it was too late. I had allowed my thoughts to go rogue, and they influenced all kinds of emotions. *Who do they think they are? How dare they try to substitute their judgment for mine? Who's leading this committee? When you lead a committee, you can do it your way.* In hindsight, I can see how I allowed thoughts of inadequacy and insecurity onto the record of my mind. What I was really thinking was, *They don't think I'm smart. They don't think I'm competent to run this committee. Maybe they're right, I can't handle this.* If I had been on the bench, I would have stricken each of those thoughts as irrelevant and not factual.

I was the subject matter expert, tapped by the presiding judge to take on this committee. Of course, I was competent. I am specifically trained in this area and thought, in advance, about how to handle this situation. Most importantly, what they thought about what I did was completely irrelevant. No one else had a complaint or concern, and it was really none of their business how I ran my meeting. I could have realized that in real-time, and responded with those rulings in mind, or not responded at all. But again, it was too late. My emotions were a runaway train and insecurity compelled me to let them know I knew what I was doing.

That resulted in a phone call that was so out of character for me. I was yelling and accusing, not even giving them a chance to speak. I have to admit—it felt good in the moment. I said some things I had rehearsed in the car on the way home. But when it was over, I just felt terrible. Instead of my colleague just thinking I could make a change in how I ran a meeting, now they thought I was a hysterical person. I was not a good representative of what a judge should be, and I was certainly not a good representative of Christ. I had not presided over my reputation very well. After two days of just stewing about it, pretending to pray about it, I had to apologize. I hate apologizing. I didn't even know if they were going to accept it or not, but I had to swallow my pride and make a genuine apology. No explanations or excuses, just an apology. What a painful lesson. Now, I no longer allow thoughts of anger, fear, insecurity, or sadness to go unchecked. I allow myself to feel all of those things, but I no longer allow them to influence my emotions to the point of dictating my behavior.

If I had been presiding, I would have remembered that whenever emotions bubble to the surface in court, that's a good time to take a recess. When a specific subject or an attorney is getting on my nerves, that is a good time to take a recess. This gives everyone a chance to cool off and gather more information, and you can gain a proper perspective before you make a ruling. When I'm sure that I'm ruling from my intellect and not from my emotions, we can resume our proceedings. When you preside, there is never a need to rule or act from your emotions. You can decide to take a recess whenever you need to.

RECESS

Have you ever been a spectator and allowed your emotions to lead you to do/say something you wish you could take back?

Journal what you were thinking, feeling, and doing the last time your emotions were in the driver's seat.

What will you do the next time you feel your emotions bubbling up?

Ideas

Our ideas also flow from the mind. There is nothing more powerful on earth than an idea. Anything and everything we can think of was produced by an idea. The chair or couch you're sitting on, your clothing, the Internet, every book you've ever read or movie you've ever seen, governments and societies—they are all born out of ideas. Great ideas outlive us. We are still pondering the ideas of Plato, Socrates, Mahatma Gandhi, and Martin Luther King Jr., to name a few. I want to invite you to start presiding over your ideas. You never know when an idea will change your life.

I keep a notebook with me wherever I go. I never know when I might hear or observe something that could turn into a great idea. I get ideas when I'm driving, while sitting in church, or while listening to music. I once had a great idea of how to approach a case while listening to a commercial on the radio. Years ago, I was presiding over a jury trial when I received the idea of presiding over my personal life. I nurtured that idea and put it into practice. That one idea is the source of this book, as well as several messages, workshops, and an online course. When you preside, you will be fruitful. I wonder how many great ideas you have just waiting to come to fruition.

RECESS

How do you preside over your ideas?
Which of your ideas has been most fruitful?

Dreams, Desires, and Disappointments

It is so important to steward our dreams and desires. Our dreams and desires can take us to our highest heights when fulfilled and take us to our deepest depths when they go unfulfilled. When we have dreams and desires, we feel excited and eager to see them come to fruition. Do everything you can to align with your dreams, even if those around you can't see it. If you preside over your dreams and desires, you will see fruit. However, when our dreams and desires aren't fulfilled or remain unfulfilled when we think they should be, we suffer disappointment. We will all be disappointed at some time in our lives. The book of Ecclesiastes tells us there is a time for everything, even disappointments. However, if you allow a season of disappointment to go on too long, it can turn into a state of bitterness. Most of the angry, sour people we encounter may have had a legitimate reason to be angry in the beginning. But because they did not preside, they allowed a season of hurt or disappointment to turn into a state of being. When you don't preside over those feelings, those feelings will begin to preside over you. How do you preside over your dreams and desires? Don't let fear hold you back. Remember, dealing with fear is in your jurisdiction. You can do something every day to prepare yourself for that dream. You can gather information by reading an article, listening to a podcast or TED Talk, or even imagining yourself in that desired state for two-to-three minutes a day.

Sidebar: Hope deferred makes the heart sick, but a dream fulfilled is a tree of life. (Proverbs 13:12 NLT)

RECESS

What dreams do you need to resurrect and preside over?
Or how can you preside over your dreams/desires?

The Wait/Taking Things Under Submission

I've talked a lot about being a steward and presiding over our jurisdiction. But I want to be clear that there are certainly times when we must simply wait. But we don't wait as a default. The Steward first determines if there is jurisdiction. If there is, she determines how to proceed, and this may include waiting. Most of the decisions I made in court were made in real-time so that the proceedings could keep moving. However, there were times when an issue came up where I wasn't quite sure about the ruling. When this happened, I could take the matter under submission. This means that I could delay my ruling until I had all the information I needed. I could have the lawyers provide more information or I could do my own research. Oftentimes, judges have discretion in their rulings. This means that there may be two or more rulings that would be lawful. So, I would have to decide which ruling was best, given all the circumstances.

These decisions were the hardest because, legally, there was no wrong answer. Sometimes, I had all the information I needed but was still uncertain about how I should rule. These tough questions also come up in our personal lives. *Should I stay with this ministry or in this relationship? Should I stay in my career or chase the dream of becoming an entrepreneur?* While the choice may result in a different experience, there may not necessarily be a wrong answer, given the circumstances. These are the times we must really be good stewards. We must first make sure that we are operating within our jurisdiction and utilizing the appropriate principles. This is also when I seek wise counsel. But sometimes there is no one or nothing with the answers we seek. It is then when we need to get quiet so we can hear any prompting from the Holy Spirit. When I do this, I wait for a sense of peace, a knowing, then I make a decision. I won't abdicate my responsibility to anyone else. A good steward understands the duty to act, but she is never in a hurry or willing to make decisions without having everything she needs.

Our Healing

"He heals the brokenhearted and binds up their wounds" (Psalm 147:3 ESV).

We all have places where we need healing. Sometimes we have experienced trauma, maybe even as children, that we are not responsible for. For example, some grew up in abusive homes or places where basic needs were neglected. If you can relate to that, you need to know that none of those things were your fault. You need to understand that you did nothing to cause those things, and you didn't deserve those things. But lovingly, I say to you, if you want to be a steward, you have to take responsibility for seeking God for your healing.

Don't waste another minute stuck blaming those who may be responsible. Back your car up and drive it straight to the only One who can heal every wound. There is nothing that you have gone through that God cannot heal, but you do have to take it to Him and be open to receive your healing. We have to acknowledge any wounding or trauma we have experienced and make a decision to forgive the person and ourselves.

Sidebar: Time does not heal all wounds. Time can only create distance between us and our wounds. We must preside and take our wounds to God, the One who can heal.

Remember, forgiveness may be a process, but the decision that we are willing to forgive is necessary. We must believe that we can be healed and take it to our God.

RECESS

What wounds can you take to God?

CHAPTER 12

Before You Take the Bench

The bench is where a judge presides. It is where she exercises her authority. If you have been following this journey, you have heeded the call, made the commitment, and donned the robe. You have learned the principles and now understand your jurisdiction. Now, you need the skill set to preside. Before you take the bench, there are a few tools that will be helpful to you.

Standing

Standing is a tool that will save you a great amount of time and energy as it will help you determine who you allow to speak into your life. There are so many influences in the world today. There used to be a limited number of influences you could consider: family, friends, and what we saw on TV or read in magazines. Today, we are bombarded with information, misinformation, and even disinformation twenty-four hours a day. People everywhere are vying for our attention, trying to tell us how we should look, what to do, what to buy, what to eat, and who to love. These influences are constantly telling us where we are falling short, and how they have the answer to fix us, as if we were broken. The number of people trying to influence us, or speak into our lives, is staggering. The principle of standing will help us discern quickly who to listen to.

Legal standing is where someone has a stake or an interest in a case before the court. Those are the only people that I allowed to be heard. Only the attorneys, litigants, and witnesses are allowed to be heard. I often hear from victims or a litigant's family and/or friends after the case has been decided. Often their goal is to persuade or influence me to make a certain decision or ruling. I never allowed mere spectators to just stand up and say whatever they wanted in my courtroom.

I've handled some very high-profile cases. In one of those cases, I made a ruling that many people were unhappy with. Normally, these types of things die down within a day or so. But in this particular case, several social media platforms were interested in this case and talk of my ruling moved like wildfire. Everyone on social media believed they had standing and could be heard, influence, or critique my rulings. Online, I was called everything but a child of God. Some made general comments, and some reached out to my personal social media accounts to express their concerns with my ruling. Some commented on my legal acumen and my intelligence. Some, without any legal background, had suggestions on how I could have handled things better. Some had sincere pleas for me to reconsider or explain my ruling. I'd be lying if I said that some of these comments weren't upsetting. However, at the end of the day, I had to remember that I make my rulings based on the law and the facts. These folks were mere spectators. Spectators take no oath and therefore have no responsibility and no power. All they can do is observe. When you preside, you cannot allow family, friends, TV, or social media to influence what you think about yourself. Don't allow these spectators to make you feel bad or guilty about where you are in life, what you have or don't have in your bank account, or even what you weigh. Make sure that you preside over yourself. Identify these spectators and treat them as such. Don't allow them standing to speak into your life. God created you and determined that you are fearfully and wonderfully made. Don't allow mere spectators in the gallery to change that.

The courtroom was created to protect the one who presides. Those who are allowed to speak or influence the judge are those who have sworn an oath and have a duty to abide by the rules. The gallery seats those who have sworn no oath and cannot even speak unless the judge allows them to. If the judge wants to hear more, she will invite only trusted participants to approach the bench or enter into chambers. We

Sidebar: A courtroom is set up to protect the one who presides. Spectators are allowed only to occupy the gallery. There is a physical bar to keep the spectator outside of the well. Only the participants, like attorneys, litigants, and jurors, are allowed closer to the judge. But it is only by invitation to the bench that a participant can get close to the judge. Consider if you're allowing mere spectators to get close enough to speak into your life.

can take a lesson from this. Don't allow those in the gallery *of your life* to have the same influence as those who are invited into chambers.

RECESS

Which Spectators have you allowed into your life?

Objections

One of the most frequently used tools by lawyers is the objection. When a lawyer makes an objection in court, they are expressing that they don't agree with what was said and they don't want that piece of evidence to be a part of the record. Lawyers love to yell out, *"Objection!"* whenever they hear anything they don't like. The judge will grant or overrule each objection. The two most common objections are, *"Objection, relevance!"* and *"Objection, hearsay!"* As a steward presiding over your life, you should always object to things that are not relevant. For example, some people like to point to past failures as a reason not to try something again. But past failures do not dictate future success. People's opinions are also not relevant and you should get used to objecting to them often. When I announced that I would retire from the bench to become an author and entrepreneur, many people voiced their opinions. Many out of genuine concern about why I would leave such a great career for something that was not as reliable or as prestigious. I could have let those opinions distract me, or I could follow that calling that was leading me to serve in a different capacity.

Lawyers object to hearsay because it is not reliable. If we do not know the source of information, it is deemed to be unreliable. Often, people, society, and social media tell us what we can and cannot do. This information is often based on what someone told them. But where did that person get the information? The only thing that is relevant and reliable is what God says about what you can be, do, or have. Object to everything else.

Striking

How do you prevent a thought from inspiring emotions and actions that take you somewhere you don't want to go? How do you keep a thought from making a nest in your head? You strike it! Every judge has this tool at her disposal. It was my favorite tool. When I was a new judge, I made a ruling in a case that I later determined to be wrong. I was mortified. I walked quickly down the hall to consult with a colleague. I poked my head into their office.

"Do you have a minute?"

He looked up at me. "Yes."

I was so upset. I just remember that I was talking fast and not really telling the story coherently. I was just rambling. Not exactly my best judicial moment.

He let me go on for a while and then he said, "So you made a ruling and you realized it was wrong?"

"Yes. What do I do?" I felt so anxious, almost desperate.

He smiled and said, "Just strike it." And then he looked back down at his papers.

I guess he thought that was the end of the conversation.

"I can just strike it. I can do that?"

"You're the judge, aren't you? You can do whatever you want. Just recall the matter and strike it. Then issue the order that you should have issued."

I just stood there. He made my colossal mistake seem so small. I said thanks and left. I was so relieved. I could just strike what was wrong and replace it with what was right.

I knew I could strike minor mistakes, like misspeaking, from the record, but I didn't realize that I could strike orders and rulings.

That's exactly what we have to do with our thoughts, beliefs, attitudes, and anything else that doesn't line up with who God has created us to be.

For example, if the thought is *I cannot do the math*, I would write that thought down. The next step is to strike that thought. I would not only draw a line through it on the paper, but I would also state out loud, "Strike that!" When I was on the bench and something entered the record in error, I declared, "Strike that!" The court reporter would dutifully strike whatever I declared should be stricken. When something is stricken, it no longer shows up on the record. It no longer exists. I do this with every errant thought that tries to pop up in my head. *I'm not good enough.* Strike that! *I can't do that.* Strike that! *I'm too old.* Strike that! When you preside, you become aware of the thoughts and beliefs that are driving your life, and so you can strike the ones that are not empowering you.

New Orders

In court, after you have stricken an order, you must replace it with a new order. This order is written in the affirmative to correct the old order. I do this with my thoughts. When I strike a thought, I write a new thought and create a new order, written in alignment with the word of God. For example, *I can do this because I am able to do all things through Christ who strengthens me. I am good enough because I am fearfully and wonderfully made.* Every time an old thought rears its ugly head, you need to strike it immediately and pronounce the new order. If you have allowed an unwanted thought to make a nest in your mind, you have the power to strike it and create a new order for your mind to obey.

RECESS

What is a persistent thought/belief and/or attitude that can you strike?
What new orders can you create to replace what was stricken?

To help with this exercise, download a copy of the Strike That Thought
Worksheet by going to: shelynabrown.com/preside-thebookworksheets

CHAPTER 13

How Do I Preside?

Now that you have the mindset, heart set—that is, the proper beliefs—and the skill set, you are ready to preside. The first thing we must preside over is our thoughts. I've talked a lot about beliefs because they determine what we do, who we are, and who we can become. If you are unhappy with where your beliefs are taking you, you can steward new beliefs. First, you have to be aware of what you really believe. Not of what you *say* you believe, but what you *really* believe.

Check Your Closet

We are guaranteed to age, but it is up to us whether or not we grow. There are many things I believed in when I was a child that I no longer believe. Thankfully, as a society, our beliefs have evolved. Not too long ago, women could not vote, buy property, or conduct business. It was believed that women did not have the intellect or the fortitude to engage in such activities. African Americans were believed to be only three-fifths of a person and were treated as such. Even the church has collectively changed some previously held beliefs. For example, when I was growing up, women in the church I attended were not allowed to wear pants or be church leaders.

There are some beliefs that we should, and will, outgrow. However, many of us never assess the beliefs we held as children. We may still believe things about ourselves or our faith that we have never looked into, to determine if these beliefs were based on something credible or even relevant. We keep those beliefs packed in our minds like a closet packed full of clothes we no longer wear. Just recently, I went through my closet and I tried on every single item. Some things no longer fit at all (thanks Covid). Some things fit, but were many years out of style. I assessed each piece, and I got rid of the items that no longer fit me or my lifestyle, even if I really liked them when I bought them. I wanted to make room for new clothes that would fit me and look good when I wore them. Every now and again, we should do this with our beliefs. Sometimes we hold on to things that don't fit, just because we love the person who gave them to us. There are many outdated ideas and church traditions that do not line up with what God's word says. For example, growing up, I always wondered why it was a sin for women to wear pants. It turns out, this was not a sin and not in the Bible, but a tradition that has since changed over time. I'm inviting you to go through your closet of beliefs and get rid of the items that are limiting, binding, and are causing you lack.

RECESS

For each belief; when/where did I acquire this belief?
Is this belief relevant?
Is this belief based on hearsay?
What is the biblical basis for this belief?

Prayers

"Therefore I tell you, whatever you ask in prayer, believe that you have received it, and it will be yours" (Mark 11:24 ESV).

Prayer is one of the most important things that we must steward. It is one spiritual practice we use to commune with God. In my introduction, I said that being a steward and understanding jurisdiction would have a profound impact on how you pray and what you ultimately pray for. Even better, it will greatly improve the effectiveness of your prayers. If you have had an unanswered prayer for years or even decades, this is for you. If you've been in church for any amount of time, you know there is nothing talked about and emphasized more than prayer. As Christians, we believe in the power of prayer. I think it is clear that prayer is something we know we should do. But how we pray determines if our prayers are effective or not. The scripture above is one of many instructions on how to pray. In that scripture, there are things that are clearly our part and there are parts that only God can do. Remember the Serenity Prayer?

God, grant me the serenity to accept the things I cannot change,
courage to change the things I can,
and wisdom to know the difference.

The things we cannot change would fall under God's jurisdiction or God's part. If you have spent any amount of time praying to impact or change things that are not in your jurisdiction, you are wasting your time. If you spend any amount of time praying for God to change the things He has given you jurisdiction over, you are wasting your time. I have heard people, in prayer, begging God for peace. Since there is an instruction on how to obtain peace, "You will keep in perfect peace all who trust in you, all whose thoughts are fixed on you!" (Isaiah 26:3 NLT), that means we have jurisdiction over our peace. Instead of *Lord give me peace*, a more effective prayer might be: *Lord, help me think about what I'm thinking about so that I can keep my mind stayed on you so that I can experience your perfect peace.*

It may not be how we are praying at all. Maybe we are not following the principle of living peaceably with others. We can't expect peace if we're stirring up trouble at home, work, and in our places of worship. The next time you're lacking peace, see if you're striving for peace with those around you (Hebrews 12:14).

We also need to know when to pray for the serenity to accept the things outside of our jurisdiction, like the past. We need to pray for the courage to preside over the things we are supposed to steward, like the present. We need to preside over our prayers for our future by asking for what it is that we want, instead of getting fixated and worrying about the things that we don't want. Understanding these distinctions will totally change your prayer life and the results you ultimately get.

Asking

Let's take a closer look at another way we can preside over our prayers. This may seem obvious, but when it comes to prayer, the first thing we are responsible for is the asking. I have prayed with many people over the years. I always ask them what they want me to pray for them. Oftentimes, they don't know exactly what they're asking God for. I've heard, *"Whatever God wants to do for me"*, or *"I just want God's will for my life"*. There's nothing necessarily wrong with this prayer, but God already knows what His will is for you.

The scripture says to ask for what *you* want. Maybe we've done something wrong and have gotten into a bad situation with our finances or a relationship we knew better than to get into. Instead of asking for what we really want, sometimes we stay and suffer as penance instead of asking for a solution or a way out. This may sound like, "*I guess this is my season or my cross to bear.*" Or maybe you have asked and have been continuously disappointed. Whatever the reason, so often we don't really ask for what we really want in prayer. I'll admit, there have been times when I didn't know what to pray for, and so praying for God's will was the best thing to pray. A young woman once asked if I would pray for her.

"What do you want me to ask God for?"

"I'm pregnant and I want the father to come back and marry me."

This seemed like a reasonable request. "Where is the father?"

"Oh, he's married. But I know he wants to be with me."

"Ok," was all I could say. I had never been stumped on a prayer request before. "Let's just pray for God's wisdom and God's will for this situation."

Seriously, I didn't know what to pray for, but I knew that praying for God's wisdom and his will for all concerned couldn't be a bad choice. I didn't want to give this young woman false hope. But, more importantly, I didn't want to pray for something contradictory to God's word. This young woman was asking me to pray that God would break up a marriage. Wisdom and peace are what I prayed— for all involved.

Not knowing what to pray for differs greatly from knowing, yet being too timid or afraid to ask for what you want. The Bible says in so many places that we are to ask God for what it is we desire (see Matthew 7:7, I John 5:15, Matthew 21:22, John 15:7, John 14:3, Mark 11:24, John 14:13-14, Matthew 7:7-11, for examples). I believe that many of us do not want to ask for so many reasons. Some of us don't ask because we don't really know what we want. We have been doing what is expected of us, yet we may not even know what it is we really want for ourselves. Some of us know what we want but are afraid to ask for it. *What if what I'm asking for makes me seem greedy, not humble, or unappreciative of what I do have? Maybe I don't even deserve what I'm asking for? What if God does not want for me what I want for me?* Whatever the reason, if we do not ask, we cannot receive. If you are not asking for what you want, you have to ask yourself, why not? I believe God gives us the desires of our hearts. If God can give to us the desires of our hearts, He can fulfill them.

In the gospel of Mark 10:46-52 (NLT), Jesus and his disciples were arriving at Jericho:

Then they reached Jericho, and as Jesus and his disciples left town, a large crowd followed him. A blind beggar named Bartimaeus (son of Timaeus) was sitting beside the road. When Bartimaeus heard that Jesus of Nazareth was nearby, he began to shout, "Jesus, Son of David, have mercy on me!"

"Be quiet!" many of the people yelled at him.

But he only shouted louder, "Son of David, have mercy on me!"

When Jesus heard him, he stopped and said, "Tell him to come here."

So they called the blind man. "Cheer up," they said. "Come on, he's calling you!" Bartimaeus threw aside his coat, jumped up, and came to Jesus.

"What do you want me to do for you?" Jesus asked.

"My Rabbi," the blind man said, "I want to see!"

And Jesus said to him, "Go, for your faith has healed you." Instantly the man could see, and he followed Jesus down the road.

Bartimaeus' vague request, "Have mercy on me," got him no result. When he responded, *"I want to see,"* to Jesus' question, "What do you want me to do?" he got a specific answer. He was immediately healed. Have you been vague in your prayers? *Lord, just bless me. I just want your will for my life.* God knows what His will is for each of us. He is asking, "What is it you want?"

What is your answer?

Recess

Do you know what it is you want to ask God for?
Are you asking for what you want? If not, why not?

Believing

Believing is the prerequisite to receiving what we pray for. We can only receive what we believe we can have. According to Mark 11:24 (NIV), believing also falls within our jurisdiction: "Therefore I tell you, whatever you ask for in prayer, believe that you have received it, and it will be yours." It is up to you to decide who or what you will allow to influence what you believe. Is it our parents, our friends, the news, social media, or statistics? It is up to us to check our closet of beliefs. We need to know what we believe and why we believe it. Don't let your beliefs be solely based on what someone else has told you. Remember, that is unreliable hearsay.

Sidebar: What would you do or say differently if you really believed that you have received what you have asked God for?

Recess

Do you truly believe what you're asking God for?
List the evidence that demonstrates this belief.

Receiving

Prayer is not one-sided. It is communion with God: speaking and listening. Often, there have been times when I didn't wait to receive what I prayed for. Instead, I made plans, trying to figure out how to make what I prayed for happen. When I couldn't see how to do this, I became discouraged and accused God of not answering my prayer. But the scripture doesn't say, *Make something happen*. It says, *Believe that you have received it, and it will be yours.*

I'm not saying that there should be no action—I just believe there should be inspired action. Receiving means, first receiving the inspiration, instruction, or idea, about what to do next. In order to do that, we must be still. We must turn off all noise and get quiet so that we can hear the instruction. Every time I released someone from jail, I gave them instructions. Oftentimes, they started asking questions or making arguments. When they did this, I said, "Sir/Ma'am, if you're talking, you can't hear me talking. Listen to my instructions, and if you still have questions, I promise I'll listen."

What they have to say may be important, but my instructions were important to their very freedom. Usually, once I'd spoken, they no longer had questions.

Every morning, I have a quiet time separate from my prayer time. During my quiet time, I'm not asking, singing, or even thanking God for what I'm asking for. I am simply sitting quietly, listening for that still small voice. When we try to make things happen on our own, without listening for that instruction, we're out of order and trying to do God's part.

Receiving is within our jurisdiction. We have to have the capacity to receive what it is we're asking for. I believe that in order to receive, we must first believe that we're worthy of receiving the blessing we're asking for. I know worthiness is a touchy subject for most of us. We were taught to be humble and not to be too greedy. I'm not saying that we are worthy because we have done something to earn it. I'm saying that because God created us, and He told us to ask. He made us worthy of what we've asked for. God could not love us any more or any less based on what we do or don't do. He simply loves us. He doesn't withdraw His love or His grace or mercy when we don't perform perfectly. That's what people do. God's love for us is unconditional. Understanding this is a big part of having the capacity to receive what you have asked for.

Recess

How often do you make time to listen for God's answers?
How do you make time to receive what you have asked for?

Capacity

Capacity is just having the space for what you have asked for. Do you remember the story in the Bible about the widow in 2 Kings 4: 4-6? She needed a way to pay her creditors so her sons wouldn't be taken away. The Prophet Elisha asked her what she had in her house. She said she only had a small amount of oil. He told her to borrow jars and vessels, as many as she could, to fill with oil. Once she began to fill the jars, the oil continued to pour. She was able to pour oil until she ran out of jars. She used that oil not just to pay her debt but, because of the abundance of oil, she and her sons were able to live on the rest.

Like this woman, we have to create the capacity to receive what we are asking for. We need to have empty vessels that can be filled with the blessings we are asking for. We may have the vessels, but I submit to you that often our vessels are already filled, leaving no room for the blessing. Whenever I'm seeking to receive something, I check to make sure that my vessels are empty. There is no room for blessings if my vessels are filled with doubt, fear, anger, or jealousy. I empty all of my vessels of anything that would hinder my blessing. When you are grateful, you are focusing on what you have instead of what someone else has. Gratitude is a great way to cleanse your vessels so that the oil can flow.

RECESS

Is anger, doubt, fear, resentment, and/or jealousy
taking up space in your vessels?
What can you do to create space for what you have
been asking God for?
What are you grateful for?

*To help with this exercise, download a copy of the Gratitude Cards
by going to: shelynabrown.com/preside-thebookworksheets*

Striking Nunc Pro Tunc

I thought that striking present mistakes was my most powerful tool as a judge. I mean, anything that does not line up with the truth of God's word, a thought, an idea, an attitude, can be erased with the words, "Strike it!" However, I discovered an even more powerful tool—striking something *Nunc Pro Tunc*. That is Latin for "now for then." This means that I have the authority to strike something from the past and erase the punishment.

A case came before me that originated before I was even a judge. It was discovered there had been a mistake in the proceedings and the punishment should not have been imposed. After some legal research, I learned I could strike the order and the punishment from the record and restore the person to where they were before the mistake was made. The person would be free of the punishment from that day forward. In addition, striking something Nunc Pro Tunc from the record wipes an order and its punishment from the record from the day it was originally signed.

That means that not only is the order stricken, but all the years of punishment associated with the old order are also stricken. The court may even order restitution to return what the person lost, to make them whole. Now, while I may be able to restore monetary loss, I can never redeem or restore the time that someone has spent in jail. But guess what? God can!

One of my best girlfriends, Angenette, told me that when she got married at fifty-two, long after she thought she would be married, she felt as though God had redeemed her time.

This is what she told me. "It wasn't until the summer of 2014, two weeks before my forty-ninth birthday, that my *special order* arrived! I'm not going to lie. I was a little hesitant at first, primarily because it had been so long, and I felt like my dating mojo had packed up and left the building. I had nagging doubts that—if I'm honest—were rooted in fear from past disappointment."

She told me she had held onto the scripture found in Joel 2:25 (DARBY). "And I will restore to you the years that the locust hath eaten, the cankerworm, and the caterpillar, and the palmer-worm, my great army which I sent among you."

"God promised to restore," she continued. "To redeem all the years of waiting, longing, and feeling forgotten and overlooked. I knew the Word, but I couldn't imagine how God would actually pull this off. I mean, *How could You possibly restore twenty-five years, Lord?* Although by outward appearances, it looks like we arrived late to the race. God was actually working it out."

"Only a few short years after our wedding, it's not uncommon for us to hear from friends and strangers alike that we seem like we've been married for decades (in the best way). I find myself giving God a little wink whenever people say 'decades.' I know now that He always had a plan to redeem every minute of that time I spent waiting, and He continues to repay it with large dividends. Best investment I've ever made."

I love this story! This is exactly what God promises for all of us. No matter how long we've waited or what it is we've waited for, God can redeem our time. It's not necessarily giving us more time, but adding life and fulfillment to the time that remains. If you are in a place where it seems that too much time has passed and your window of opportunity has closed, I want to encourage you that it has not! Even if things have not been fruitful for quite some time, God always has the last say over time. No matter what it is, remember that time is in God's jurisdiction. He can redeem the time it feels that you have lost. If you want to go back to school, start that business or ministry, find that love or anything else, God can redeem the time for us to fully live our dreams.

I started thinking about this when it came to beliefs that no longer serve me. You know which beliefs I'm talking about: the beliefs that say you're too old or too young to try something different. The beliefs that tell you that no one who looks like you is doing this or that, so you can't either. Any belief that is no longer true or empowering should be examined. For example, for years, I was taught that a woman could not be called to ministry. In the church I grew up in, a woman could teach from the floor, but she was not allowed in the pulpit. When I went away to college, I visited a church with a friend. His mother, Dr. Cynthia James, was the pastor. I was intrigued. Not only was she a preacher, but she was a pastor. I'd never seen or heard of that before. I couldn't wait to see what a woman preacher would look and sound like. She was incredible. I was mesmerized the minute she opened her mouth. It was sound teaching, substantive, and entertaining. I couldn't shake that experience. It was in direct conflict with what I believed a woman could do in the church.

Years later, when I received that unmistakable call to ministry, I didn't know what to do. Old beliefs about how I was raised crept back in. What would people at home think? Would people really believe God had called me? Did I really believe God had called me? I ignored it and tried to suppress it because I did not believe it was possible, at least not for me. Despite seeing many amazing women in ministry (Priscilla Shirer, Beth Moore, Dr. Cynthia James, and so many others), I realized I still maintained an underlying belief that women could not be called to preach and teach the gospel.

Sometimes, our beliefs are not readily apparent. Sometimes we say we believe something, but what we say we believe is not evident in our lives. I said I believed women could be called to a teaching/preaching ministry, but I would not accept the call to ministry because deep down, I didn't believe it for me. You may say that you believe you can do all things through Christ who strengthens you: "For I can do everything through Christ, who gives me strength" (Philippians 4:13 NLT). However, you keep putting off the things you have a desire to do. You won't start that business, or ministry, or put yourself out there to find love because you've been hurt.

In court, when a litigant wants to talk to a person who is reluctant to talk, they may have to subpoena them. This means they can use the authority of the court to demand that person show themselves in court for examination. Beliefs are somewhat like this. Some beliefs are so old and deep-rooted that we don't even know they are there. Like my belief about women in ministry. Sometimes you must subpoena those beliefs and command them to show themselves.

Some beliefs are only revealed after prayer, meditation, or fasting. You may need the wise counsel of a trusted friend, counselor, or coach to help you reveal these beliefs. Once this belief is revealed, examine it. Is it true? Is it relevant? Is it serving you? Does it need to be amended? Does it need to be stricken? If they need to be stricken, you (yes, you!) must strike them nunc pro tunc. Strike them from the root so that they do not return. Once they are stricken, you are not only free from that belief, but free from the punishment that belief was rendered.

RECESS

What old beliefs, attitudes, hurts, or resentments need to be stricken nunc pro tunc?
You can download a free worksheet for this exercise, which goes through this process in detail, from my website: www.shelynabrown.com

CHAPTER 14

Summation

I wrote this book hoping to convince you of the benefits of becoming a good steward over everything that God has entrusted to you. That an abundant and fruitful life is the life that God wants for you. I wanted to enlighten you about the jurisdiction God created for you, with the hope that you would begin to surrender to the things you cannot change, use your time and energy on the things that you can change, and give you the tools to know the difference. I wanted to encourage you to learn and exercise God's principles to move beyond lack and stagnation and understand that lack is not a result of God's will or His timing. I wanted to empower you to accept the authority that you have been given by God, in the hope that you will use it to create the life you really want and not just settle for the life you have. I wanted to share the awesome power of stewardship and how it has helped me to preside over my own life.

I also wanted to share that no matter where we are, no matter what we have done or not done, we can decide to be a good steward and God can restore us and redeem our time. I wanted to remind you that Jesus came so that we might have life, and have it more abundantly, and that He showed us in His word how to do so. My prayer for you is that you begin to see yourself as God sees you:

a capable steward, worthy of the most abundant life that you will allow yourself to receive. I hope that you begin to see God for who He really is—a kind and loving God who is always waiting to receive you exactly the way you are. There is not one thing you could ever do to make God love you any more than He already does.

One last thing. My favorite thing as a judge was to say, "It is so ordered." Once I say this, lawyers know that there is nothing more to be said and what I have said has become an order and must be followed. If you accept the call, take the oath, learn the principles, don the robe, and know and exercise your authority within your jurisdiction, you can preside over every area of your life. You can ask anything, and

> **Sidebar: "You did not choose me, but I chose you and appointed you so that you might go and bear fruit—fruit that will last—and so that whatever you ask in my name the Father will give you" (John 15:16 NIV).**

if you believe it, you can receive it. If you're ready for a life of abundance—take authority, know *your* jurisdiction, think it, speak it, act on it, believe it, and preside over it. It is so ordered!

CONTACT THE AUTHOR

If you would like further information or support
to help you *Preside*, please visit my website:
www.shelynabrown.com

Prayer of Salvation

Jesus,

I believe that through Your death and resurrection, You destroyed the power of sin, evil, and permanent death once and for all. I accept Your everlasting grace, ever-present forgiveness, and Lordship over my life and destiny forever!

Amen.

—prayer by Pastor Hurman Hamilton

Biblical Instructions on How to Address Our Emotions

Note: The following Biblical citations are all from the English Standard Version (ESV).

Anger

Proverbs 14:29
"Whoever is slow to anger has great understanding, but he who has a hasty temper exalts folly."

Psalm 37:8
"Refrain from anger, and forsake wrath! Fret not yourself; it tends only to evil."

Proverbs 15:1
"A soft answer turns away wrath, but a harsh word stirs up anger."

James 1:20
"For the anger of man does not produce the righteousness of God."

Ephesians 4:26
"Be angry and do not sin; do not let the sun go down on your anger,"

James 1:19
"Know this, my beloved brothers: let every person be quick to hear, slow to speak, slow to anger;"

Ecclesiastes 7:9
"Be not quick in your spirit to become angry, for anger lodges in the heart of fools."

Proverbs 29:11
"A fool gives full vent to his spirit, but a wise man quietly holds it back."

Proverbs 19:11
"Good sense makes one slow to anger, and it is his glory to overlook an offense".

Anxious/Overwhelmed

Philippians 4:6-7
"Do not be anxious about anything, but in everything by prayer and supplication with thanksgiving let your requests be made known to God. And the peace of God, which surpasses all understanding, will guard your hearts and your minds in Christ Jesus."

1 Peter 5:7
"Casting all your anxieties on him, because he cares for you."

Fear

2 Timothy 1:7
"For God gave us a spirit not of fear but of power and love and self-control."

1 John 4:18
"There is no fear in love, but perfect love casts out fear. For fear has to do with punishment, and whoever fears has not been perfected in love."

Psalm 34:4
"I sought the LORD, and he answered me and delivered me from all my fears."

Joshua 1:9
"Have I not commanded you? Be strong and courageous. Do not be frightened, and do not be dismayed, for the LORD your God is with you wherever you go."

Depression

Psalm 34:17-18
"When the righteous cry for help, the LORD hears and delivers them out of all their troubles. The LORD is near to the brokenhearted and saves the crushed in spirit."

2 Corinthians 7:6
"But God, who comforts the downcast, comforted us by the coming of Titus."

Isaiah 41:10
"Fear not, for I am with you; be not dismayed, for I am your God; I will strengthen you, I will help you, I will uphold you with my righteous right hand."

1 Peter 5:7
"Casting all your anxieties on him, because he cares for you."

Matthew 11:28
"Come to me, all who labor and are heavy laden, and I will give you rest."

Jeremiah 29:11
"For I know the plans I have for you, declares the LORD, plans for welfare and not for evil, to give you a future and a hope."

Proverbs 3:5-6
"Trust in the LORD with all your heart, and do not lean on your own understanding. In all your ways acknowledge him, and he will make straight your paths."

Psalm 143:7-8

"Answer me quickly, O LORD! My spirit fails! Hide not your face from me, lest I be like those who go down to the pit. Let me hear in the morning of your steadfast love, for in you I trust. Make me know the way I should go, for to you I lift up my soul."

Psalm 30:5

"For his anger is but for a moment, and his favor is for a lifetime. Weeping may tarry for the night, but joy comes with the morning."

Philippians 4:6-7

"Do not be anxious about anything, but in everything by prayer and supplication with thanksgiving let your requests be made known to God. And the peace of God, which surpasses all understanding, will guard your hearts and your minds in Christ Jesus."

Jealousy/Envy

James 3:16

"For where jealousy and selfish ambition exist, there will be disorder and every vile practice."

1 Corinthians 3:3

"For you are still of the flesh. For while there is jealousy and strife among you, are you not of the flesh and behaving only in a human way?"

Galatians 5:19-21

"Now the works of the flesh are evident: sexual immorality, impurity, sensuality, idolatry, sorcery, enmity, strife, jealousy, fits of anger, rivalries, dissensions, divisions, envy, drunkenness, orgies, and things like these. I warn you, as I warned you before, that those who do such things will not inherit the kingdom of God."

Exodus 20:17

"You shall not covet your neighbor's house; you shall not covet your neighbor's wife, or his male servant, or his female servant, or his ox, or his donkey, or anything that is your neighbor's."

Job 5:2
"Surely vexation kills the fool, and jealousy slays the simple."

Proverbs 6:34
"For jealousy makes a man furious, and he will not spare when he takes revenge."

Proverbs 14:30
"A tranquil heart gives life to the flesh, but envy makes the bones rot."

Joy

Romans 15:13
"May the God of hope fill you with all joy and peace in believing, so that by the power of the Holy Spirit you may abound in hope."

Philippians 4:4
"Rejoice in the Lord always; again I will say, rejoice."

James 1:2
"Count it all joy, my brothers, when you meet trials of various kinds,"

Galatians 5:22
"But the fruit of the Spirit is love, joy, peace, patience, kindness, goodness, faithfulness,"

Psalm 16:11
"You make known to me the path of life; in your presence there is fullness of joy; at your right hand are pleasures forevermore."

John 16:24
"Until now you have asked nothing in my name. Ask, and you will receive, that your joy may be full."

Proverbs 17:22
"A joyful heart is good medicine, but a crushed spirit dries up the bones."

Peace

John 16:33
"I have said these things to you, that in me you may have peace. In the world you will have tribulation. But take heart; I have overcome the world."

Isaiah 26:3
"You keep him in perfect peace whose mind is stayed on you, because he trusts in you."

Matthew 5:9
"Blessed are the peacemakers, for they shall be called sons of God."

Philippians 4:6
"Do not be anxious about anything, but in everything by prayer and supplication with thanksgiving let your requests be made known to God."

John 14:27
"Peace I leave with you; my peace I give to you. Not as the world gives do I give to you. Let not your hearts be troubled, neither let them be afraid."

Romans 12:18
"If possible, so far as it depends on you, live peaceably with all."

Sadness/Depression

Psalm 34:18
"The LORD is near to the brokenhearted and saves the crushed in spirit."

John 14:1
"Let not your hearts be troubled. Believe in God; believe also in me."

Psalm 55:22
"Cast your burden on the LORD, and he will sustain you; he will never permit the righteous to be moved."

Jeremiah 29:11
"For I know the plans I have for you, declares the LORD, plans for welfare and not for evil, to give you a future and a hope."

Psalm 34:17-18
"When the righteous cry for help, the LORD hears and delivers them out of all their troubles. The LORD is near to the brokenhearted and saves the crushed in spirit."

2 Corinthians 7:6
"But God, who comforts the downcast, comforted us by the coming of Titus,"

Biblical Principles/Instructions on How to Preside over Every Area of Our Lives

Note: The following Biblical citations are all from the English Standard Version (ESV).

Forgiveness

Ephesians 4:32
"Be kind to one another, tenderhearted, forgiving one another, as God in Christ forgave you."

Mark 11:25
"And whenever you stand praying, forgive, if you have anything against anyone, so that your Father also who is in heaven may forgive you your trespasses."

Matthew 6:15
"But if you do not forgive others their trespasses, neither will your Father forgive your trespasses."

Faithfulness

Proverbs 28:20
"A faithful man will abound with blessings, but whoever hastens to be rich will not go unpunished."

Luke 16:10-12
"One who is faithful in a very little is also faithful in much, and one who is dishonest in a very little is also dishonest in much. If then you have not been faithful in the unrighteous wealth, who will entrust to you the true riches? And if you have not been faithful in that which is another's, who will give you that which is your own?"

2 Corinthians 5:7
"For we walk by faith, not by sight."

Fear

Isaiah 41:10
"Fear not, for I am with you; be not dismayed, for I am your God; I will strengthen you, I will help you, I will uphold you with my righteous right hand."

2 Timothy 1:7
"For God gave us a spirit not of fear but of power and love and self-control."

1 John 4:18
"There is no fear in love, but perfect love casts out fear. For fear has to do with punishment, and whoever fears has not been perfected in love."

Psalm 34:4
"I sought the LORD, and he answered me and delivered me from all my fears."

Giving/Tithing

Malachi 3:8-10
Will man rob God? Yet you are robbing me. But you say, 'How have we robbed you?' In your tithes and contributions. You are cursed with a curse, for you are robbing me, the whole nation of you. Bring the full tithe into the storehouse, that there may be food in my house. And thereby put me to the test, says the LORD of hosts, if I will not open the windows of heaven for you and pour down for you a blessing until there is no more need.

Proverbs 3:9
"Honor the LORD with your wealth and with the first fruits of all your produce"

2 Corinthians 9:7
"Each one must give as he has decided in his heart, not reluctantly or under compulsion, for God loves a cheerful giver."

Gratitude

1 Thessalonians 5:18
"Give thanks in all circumstances; for this is the will of God in Christ Jesus for you."

Psalm 118:24
"This is the day that the LORD has made; let us rejoice and be glad in it."

Psalm 136:1
"Give thanks to the LORD, for he is good, for his steadfast love endures forever."

Psalm 107:1
"Oh give thanks to the LORD, for he is good, for his steadfast love endures forever!"

Healing

Jeremiah 17:14
"Heal me, O LORD, and I shall be healed; save me, and I shall be saved, for you are my praise."

Psalm 41:3
"The LORD sustains him on his sickbed; in his illness you restore him to full health."

Ecclesiastes 3:1-8
"For everything there is a season, and a time for every matter under heaven: a time to be born, and a time to die; a time to plant, and a time to pluck up what is planted; a time to kill, and a time to heal; a time to break down, and a time to build up; a time to weep, and a time to laugh; a time to mourn, and a time to dance; a time to cast away stones, and a time to gather stones together; a time to embrace, and a time to refrain from embracing; a time to seek, and a time to lose; a time to keep, and a time to cast away; a time to tear, and a time to sew; a time to keep silence, and a time to speak; a time to love, and a time to hate; a time for war, and a time for peace."

Humility

Proverbs 22:4
"The reward for humility and fear of the LORD is riches and honor and life."

Proverbs 11:2
"When pride comes, then comes disgrace, but with the humble is wisdom."

James 4:10
"Humble yourselves before the Lord, and he will exalt you."

Joy

Philippians 4:4
"Rejoice in the Lord always; again I will say, rejoice."

James 1:2
"Count it all joy, my brothers, when you meet trials of various kinds,"

John 16:24
"Until now you have asked nothing in my name. Ask, and you will receive, that your joy may be full."

Proverbs 17:22
"A joyful heart is good medicine, but a crushed spirit dries up the bones."

Psalm 30:5
"For his anger is but for a moment, and his favor is for a lifetime. Weeping may tarry for the night, but joy comes with the morning."

Love

1 Corinthians 16:4
"If it seems advisable that I should go also, they will accompany me."

1 John 4:8
"Anyone who does not love does not know God, because God is love."

1 Peter 4:8
"Above all, keep loving one another earnestly, since love covers a multitude of sins."

Colossians 3:14
"And above all these put on love, which binds everything together in perfect harmony."

John 13:34-35
"A new commandment I give to you, that you love one another: just as I have loved you, you also are to love one another. By this all people will know that you are my disciples, if you have love for one another."

Meditation

Psalm 1:2
"But his delight is in the law of the LORD, and on his law he meditates day and night."

Psalm 119:15
"I will meditate on your precepts and fix my eyes on your ways."

Psalm 19:14
"Let the words of my mouth and the meditation of my heart be acceptable in your sight, O Lord, my rock and my redeemer."

Psalm 119:97
"Oh how I love your law! It is my meditation all the day."

Philippians 4:8
"Finally, brothers, whatever is true, whatever is honorable, whatever is just, whatever is pure, whatever is lovely, whatever is commendable, if there is any excellence, if there is anything worthy of praise, think about these things."

Peace

Isaiah 26:3
"You keep him in perfect peace whose mind is stayed on you, because he trusts in you."

John 14:27
"Peace I leave with you; my peace I give to you. Not as the world gives do I give to you. Let not your hearts be troubled, neither let them be afraid."

Romans 12:18
"If possible, so far as it depends on you, live peaceably with all."

Hebrews 12:14
"Strive for peace with everyone, and for the holiness without which no one will see the Lord."

1 Peter 5:7
"Casting all your anxieties on him, because he cares for you."

Prayer

Jude 1:20
"But you, beloved, building yourselves up in your most holy faith and praying in the Holy Spirit,"

1 Thessalonians 5:17
"Pray without ceasing,"

John 15:7
"If you abide in me, and my words abide in you, ask whatever you wish, and it will be done for you."

Colossians 4:2
"Continue steadfastly in prayer, being watchful in it with thanksgiving."

Reaping/Sowing

2 Corinthians 9:6-8
The point is this: whoever sows sparingly will also reap sparingly, and whoever sows bountifully will also reap bountifully. Each one must give as he has decided in his heart,not reluctantly or under compulsion, for God loves a cheerful giver. And God is able to make all grace abound to you, so that having all sufficiency in all things at all times, you may abound in every good work."

Luke 6:38
"Give, and it will be given to you. Good measure, pressed down, shaken together, running over, will be put into your lap. For with the measure you use it will be measured back to you."

Sadness

John 14:1
"Let not your hearts be troubled. Believe in God; believe also in me."

Jeremiah 29:11
"For I know the plans I have for you, declares the LORD, plans for welfare and not for evil, to give you a future and a hope."

John 10:10
"The thief comes only to steal and kill and destroy. I came that they may have life and have it abundantly."

Self-Control

Proverbs 25:28
"A man without self-control is like a city broken into and left without walls."

Titus 1:8
"But hospitable, a lover of good, self-controlled, upright, holy, and disciplined."

Stewardship

Genesis 1:28
"And God blessed them. And God said to them, 'Be fruitful and multiply and fill the earth and subdue it, and have dominion over the fish of the sea and over the birds of the heavens and over every living thing that moves on the earth.'"

1 Peter 4:10
"As each has received a gift, use it to serve one another, as good stewards of God's varied grace"

1 Corinthians 4:2
"Moreover, it is required of stewards that they be found faithful."

The Body

1 Corinthians 3:16
"Do you not know that you are God's temple and that God's Spirit dwells in you?"

1 Corinthians 6:19
"Or do you not know that your body is a temple of the Holy Spirit within you, whom you have from God? You are not your own,"

The Holy Spirit

John 14:26
"But the Helper, the Holy Spirit, whom the Father will send in my name, he will teach you all things and bring to your remembrance all that I have said to you."

Romans 8:26
"Likewise the Spirit helps us in our weakness. For we do not know what to pray for as we ought, but the Spirit himself intercedes for us with groanings too deep for words."

Romans 8:28
"And we know that for those who love God all things work together for good, for those who are called according to his purpose."

John 4:24
"God is spirit, and those who worship him must worship in spirit and truth."

The Mind

Romans 12:2
"Do not be conformed to this world, but be transformed by the renewal of your mind, that by testing you may discern what is the will of God, what is good and acceptable and perfect."

Philippians 2:5
"Have this mind among yourselves, which is yours in Christ Jesus"

Philippians 4:8-9
"Finally, brothers, whatever is true, whatever is honorable, whatever is just, whatever is pure, whatever is lovely, whatever is commendable, if there is any excellence, if there is anything worthy of praise, think about these things. What you have learned and received and heard

and seen in me—practice these things, and the God of peace will be with you."

2 Corinthians 10:5
"We destroy arguments and every lofty opinion raised against the knowledge of God, and take every thought captive to obey Christ"

The Tongue

Proverbs 18:21
"Death and life are in the power of the tongue, and those who love it will eat its fruits."

James 1:26
"If anyone thinks he is religious and does not bridle his tongue but deceives his heart, this person's religion is worthless."

1 Peter 3:10
"For whoever desires to love life and see good days, let him keep his tongue from evil and his lips from speaking deceit"

Time

Ecclesiastes 3:1
"For everything there is a season, and a time for every matter under heaven."

Joel 2:25
"I will restore to you the years that the swarming locust has eaten, the hopper, the destroyer, and the cutter, my great army, which I sent among you."

Past

Ecclesiastes 7:10
"Say not, 'Why were the former days better than these?' For it is not from wisdom that you ask this."

Philippians 3:13-14
"Brothers, I do not consider that I have made it my own. But one thing I do: forgetting what lies behind and straining forward to what lies ahead, I press on toward the goal for the prize of the upward call of God in Christ Jesus."

Present

Isaiah 43:18-19
 "Remember not the former things, nor consider the things of old. Behold, I am doing a new thing; now it springs forth, do you not perceive it? I will make a way in the wilderness and rivers in the desert."

Future

Matthew 6:25
"Therefore I tell you, do not be anxious about your life, what you will eat or what you will drink, nor about your body, what you will put on. Is not life more than food, and the body more than clothing?"

Matthew 6:34
"Therefore do not be anxious about tomorrow, for tomorrow will be anxious for itself. Sufficient for the day is its own trouble."

Psalm 55:22
"Cast your burden on the LORD, and he will sustain you; he will never permit the righteous to be moved."

Philippians 4:19
"And my God will supply every need of yours according to his riches in glory in Christ Jesus."

Luke 12:25
"And which of you by being anxious can add a single hour to his span of life?"

REFERENCES

Craig, Anne, 2020. "Discovery of 'thought worms' opens window to the mind." Queen's Gazette. 13th July https://www.queensu.ca/gazette/stories/discovery-thought-worms-opens-window-mind

Leaf, Caroline. 2015. *Switch On Your Brain: The Key to Peak Happiness, Thinking, and Health*. Michigan. Baker Books.

ABOUT THE AUTHOR

Judge Shelyna Brown is a distinguished retired judge, a seasoned minister, adjunct professor, mentor, and an influential executive coach and trainer for lawyers and judges. Her unwavering commitment to justice, equality, and service has left an indelible mark on multiple facets of the legal and spiritual landscapes.

Born and raised in Fresno, CA, Shelyna's passion for justice was ignited at a young age as she witnessed first-hand inequalities in her own neighborhood. She pursued her undergraduate degree at UC Davis and obtained her juris doctorate from Santa Clara University, School of Law. She carved her initial niche in the  Office of the Public Defender, where she blossomed as a formidable attorney with her adept legal prowess and compassionate approach.

She ascended to the bench where she served with distinction, as a Superior Court Judge until her retirement in 2023. Shelyna continues to serve her community as an adjunct professor, speaker, and trainer for law students, lawyers, and judges.

Encountering Shelyna Brown is to witness a living narrative of inspiration and hope. Her journey is a testament to a commitment of service empowering leadership and a transformative impact that transcends boundaries.

Shelyna lives in San Jose, CA with her husband, Alan Hamilton.

Made in the USA
Las Vegas, NV
14 March 2024

87140409R00108